The Real Man's
GUIDE TO DIVORCE

JAMES BRIEN

ISBN: 978-1-9161418-0-3

First published in 2019

As part of this product you have also received FREE access to parenting plans and financial tools to help you through your divorce.

To gain access, simply go to:

www.freedivorceadvice.co.uk

For more advice and support to help you with your divorce or separation visit:

www.realmansdivorce.com

To Phoebe and Rafe – Dance to
the beat of your own drum.

CONTENTS

PREFACE

The early days in an empty house, devoid of the buzz of family life, were tough. Like many men, I rarely allowed my feelings to feature heavily in my life. When they did surface, I never let them stick around for long.

I was a creature of logic. In my mind, any situation could be overcome by thinking logically and taking action.

On the first weekend I found myself alone, I was living in Grange-Over-Sands, a little village sandwiched between the sea and the mountains of the Lake District in Northern England. I was miles away from friends, book shops or any other resource that could assist with my logical analysis of the situation.

Being left alone with my thoughts felt miserable, so I did what any sensible person would do. I dug out my Ordnance Survey map, plotted a route and set off on a gruelling four-hour run with music blasting in my headphones to drown out any thoughts. The goal was to exhaust myself so that I was too tired to think, and it worked.

I was too drained to go running again the next day, so logic kicked back in. I knew that almost half of all marriages end in divorce, so I assumed that there would be loads of useful advice on the internet.

After a quick search, I learned that 60% of second marriages and over 70% of third marriages end in divorce as well. I discovered that Mel Gibson paid $425 million in his divorce settlement, and I made a mental note to avoid this. Then, I felt a flicker of achievement. Britney Spears held the record for the shortest marriage of 56 hours. I'd managed to beat this by several years.

But, my optimism was short-lived. The majority of the advice available online was terrible. I found many forums on divorce, but their content consisted primarily of angry and emotional rants. It is hard to think of any other scenario that creates so much hostility between men and women. In both male and female forums, I could feel the venom leap from the screen.

This was the last thing I needed. What I wanted was clear guidance to help me navigate this unstable time in my life.

I wrote this book because I had no one to turn to for advice when I went through my divorce. Despite the high rate of divorce, I could only think of one friend who had been through it, and he lived in Spain. The only real source of knowledge comes from experience, so friends who hadn't been through it struggled to help despite their best efforts.

My number one priority during this separation was to make sure that my two wonderful children were okay and that I saw them regularly.

My second priority concerned money. In my career, I'd spent a lot of time and money on lawyers. I'd seen first-hand how conflicts made their cash register sing. I didn't want to get into lengthy legal arguments with my wife and blow all of our money.

These two main objectives, to make sure that my children were okay and to not waste money on solicitors, helped me focus on finding the best way forward.

This book is a no-nonsense guide to making the best out of your separation or divorce. It is written primarily for men, because there is a lack of useful resources for them. Most books on divorce are written by women for women, but men usually have different needs and concerns.

Rather than tackle only the obvious challenges like legal divorce, access to children and finances, I want to make sure that we cover mental and physical wellbeing as well. This is a tough time, and, as with any highly charged situation, you need to be in top form. Yet, due to the very nature of this situation, you are unlikely to be playing at your best, and you will certainly have bad days. In these circumstances, it is easy to make some huge mistakes and end up feeling worse.

I want to show you how to make the very best of this situation. I will show you how to come through it stronger, happier and healthier. It might seem impossible to you right now, but I know from experience that if you follow the processes in this book, you will feel better. You owe it to yourself to be in the best possible position to deal with the challenges ahead.

In the interest of full disclosure, I should make it clear that I am not on the side of men or women. In fact, where children are involved, I'm picking up the mantle for them. Children benefit from having two parents to guide them, support them and love them. Being separated from a parent is extremely difficult for a child. I ask you to think about how you would feel if you never saw your child again. Hold on to that feeling for a moment. This is how your child will feel at least some of the time following separation. And do you know who can either intensify or ease that feeling? The parents.

My aim is to provide a guide that is sensible and fair to all parties. I want to minimise conflict. I want each parent to feel happier and stronger and to be closer to their children following separation. Children do what they see us do, rather than what we tell them to do. We owe it to them to be the best version of ourselves and to be role models irrespective of the situation we find ourselves in.

I hope you find this book helpful and that you put its ideas to good use. Please let me know your comments, feedback and success stories at james@realmansdivorce.com. With your permission, I will use them in later editions of the book to benefit other readers.

Five percent of the profits from this book will go to charities that help disadvantaged children have the best start in life.

James Brien April 2019.

INTRODUCTION

Separation is the end of a relationship between two people. Regardless of who initiated it, who wants it and who doesn't, or whether it was a mutual decision, it hurts. However, the way you handle yourself post-split will be the key to your recovery.

The flood of emotions and feelings that you will experience is unlike anything else. These feelings will rush in and out and vary in intensity. You may feel despair, anger, sadness, a sense of being lost or a lack of motivation. You may feel a physical ache in your stomach that will not subside. You may feel extremely sensitive, and everything may remind you of your ex-partner or your children. All of these feelings are natural, but this doesn't provide much solace.

But there is good news. All of these feelings will subside over time and eventually go away. The key word here is time, but you can also be proactive to facilitate the healing process. If you start on a dark path of self-destruction, however, it will only take more time to heal, and you will hurt for longer than necessary.

It is understandable to want to numb the pain and perhaps drink in excess. However, this will only make matters worse. Alcohol is a depressant; it will bring your mood down. Everything will feel worse, especially when that hangover kicks in. This is when you really start beating on yourself: Is it just me? Will I ever find anyone again? Am I destined to a life of misery? Avoid this place as much as possible, and steer clear of alcohol and other drugs.

Do not isolate yourself either. This is the time that you need to be around people who love and care about you, people who will build you up and support you. Being alone, overthinking and reminiscing achieve nothing.

If nothing else, get out of the house and go for a walk or, even better, a run or a jog. Exercise causes your body to release endorphins, the feel-good chemicals that raise your mood and put you in a more resourceful state of mind.

Avoid sleeping around. I know it feels good and takes your mind off of your situation, especially in the heat of the moment. But the next day, you are likely to feel even more empty. Even worse, you might end up rebounding and getting into a new relationship prematurely.

While our goal is to get over the heartbreak and move on, I'm a firm believer in doing this ourselves. We must deal with our emotions and not distract ourselves by finding a new relationship. Look at your separation as an opportunity to learn about yourself.

None of us are perfect human beings, so it is likely that you contributed to your separation in some way. This book will help you identify and deal with your mistakes in order to avoid making those same mistakes twice. Entering a new relationship before completing this process will likely lead to the same outcome.

Pain is not something that we should continually run from or shut out. Nor is it something that we should embrace and hold on to. Pain usually teaches us something, so recognise your pain, learn from it and let it go.

The pain that you are feeling will dwindle and ultimately go away, but this process does take time. My hope for you is that you start working on yourself. This is the time for you to develop yourself and build up your confidence. It is time to take care of yourself.

You have nobody else to please but yourself. Consider giving yourself a total image overhaul. Buy a different wardrobe, get a new haircut and start working out. Take up some new hobbies. Do things that you want to do. Become more aware of who you are, what is important to you and what you stand for.

When you start working on yourself like this, you will find that as your confidence rises, your pain will subside. With higher confidence, everything gets better. You will be in a great place emotionally, and you will attract beautiful experiences and people into your life.

There is no hiding from the fact that separation hurts. But if you set yourself up for failure by pressing the self-destruct button, the pain will increase and last much longer than necessary. By taking care of yourself, developing your confidence and enhancing your self-worth, you will bounce back more quickly. I promise. This is how a real man handles divorce and separation.

Planning the Divorce

It might sound cold and calculating, but when children are involved, it is better to prepare your separation in advance, rather than letting it play out in the heat of the moment. A blazing row before leaving the house can be very traumatic, especially for children. Separation is always stressful, but you can reduce this stress with a plan.

Once you have reached the decision to separate, you need to agree on significant decisions about living arrangements, access to children and financial arrangements.

Children want to know where the parent who is moving out is going to live. This home needs to be as appropriate for children as the finances allow, and it needs to be ready for their visit. Agreeing on how much time your child will spend with each of you could be a challenge.

Financial details will need immediate attention as well. Joint bank accounts should be closed and responsibility for bills agreed upon. Temporary support payments should be put in place, and temporary decisions need to be made on shared assets, such as who gets the car and which furniture will be split.

I remember giving up most of our furniture except for a pink occasion chair. I had to sit in that chair for three months while waiting for my sofa to arrive. I was thankful, though, that I only had to sleep on a blow-up bed for two weeks until my bed was delivered. The key to coping with separation is to put the needs of the children first, be flexible and keep a sense of humour.

Personal issues need to be addressed. First, you need to decide who to tell about the separation and what you will say to them. After your child, you need to tell your parents, friends, neighbours, teachers and colleagues. The timing is up to you.

Women tend to share quickly, but I took my time. I didn't tell some people for months. So long, in fact, that it became difficult to raise the subject after so much time had passed.

Separation is a stressful time. Several matters will need immediate attention while many others will not. Take your time. Postpone and delay as much as possible. Even if you think you are feeling okay, there is a chance that you are not 100%. You might look back on some of the hasty decisions you made during this time and wish you had handled them differently.

What follows in this book are tools and techniques not only to help you in the short term, but also to support you in your future life. I hope that you will look back on this moment in your life and recognise it as a turning point, a pivotal time when you learned how to lead a happier life and develop and nurture better relationships.

CHAPTER 2:
DEVELOPING YOUR INNER GAME

During the second edit of this book, my job was made redundant. Up to that point, I'd been working on the book early in the mornings, late in the evenings and on the weekends. Now I had the perfect opportunity to finish the book. But what did i do? Anything but, and progress was slow.

I was eating poorly, not looking after myself and gaining weight. I was becoming increasingly frustrated with myself and feeling fed up in general. My mood kept dropping until, eventually, the penny dropped.

I wasn't practicing any of the processes that follow in this chapter, techniques that I knew from experience actually worked. I asked myself: How am I writing this book and not following my own advice?

And then it came to me as it will come to you. We know what is good for us, we know what we must do, but we fail to act. We fail to act, because we haven't reached our breaking point yet. We haven't reached the point where we say: *Enough is enough. I'm not taking this anymore.*

The feelings we go through when we separate from our partner are similar to, though less intense than, those we experience when we've been made redundant. I had reached my breaking point, and I was sick of it. At that point, I got out my journal and threw myself into the exercises that follow. I committed myself to the process, and it worked. My wish is that you find the strength to do the same.

Managing Stress

Divorce is a process that takes time. My divorce was relatively quick, but it still took almost two years from the initial separation to receiving the decree absolute. The specifics of each divorce are unique, but we all tend to go through a similar set of emotions.

It is helpful to remember that you are not the only person who is facing divorce and its slew of difficult emotions.

Understandably, many people experience a deep sense of loneliness. You will likely replay scenarios and decisions over and over in your head. You might ask yourself: What if I had done things differently? Would that have saved the marriage? Am I doing the right thing? Is there anything else I can do?

You will feel anger and, of course, sadness. Special days such as birthdays and Christmas can increase the intensity of such emotions, especially if access to your children is restricted in some way. Despite this, you must remember that these feelings are normal. It is a process, an emotional roller coaster that will eventually stop. For now, while you are on the ride, the best you can do is keep calm and take care of yourself.

It is critical to look after yourself physically and mentally during this process. Let us start by looking at how you can manage stress, because how you cope with stress will have a significant impact on your overall wellbeing.

There are three basic coping strategies for managing stress:

1. Solution-Focused: Doing something to manage or change a situation
2. Emotion-Focused: Managing your emotional response to a situation rather than changing the situation
3. Avoidance-Focused: Ignoring or refusing to accept a situation or distracting yourself from it

Clearly, the avoidance style is not helpful and could lead to further problems, especially if alcohol is used as a distraction. If you are faced with a situation that you can change, a solution-focused approach will likely work best. However, if you are dealing with a situation that is out of your control, an emotion-focused response will be your best option.

In divorce, as in life, there are some things that you can control and some things that you cannot. For example, you have little control over your ex-partner's behaviour. But, you have full control of how you react to her, and you can use the emotion-focused approach successfully so that her actions do not negatively affect your mood.

How you manage stress is essential for you and your children. The more stressed you become, the less effective you will be in all aspects of your life. For instance, you wouldn't want to fly off the handle at work and jeopardise your job. If you have children, they will sense your stress, and your number one objective right now is to take care of them and shield them from negative energy.

We all experience stress in our lives, and some stress can be helpful, but when it builds to the point where it's affecting our ability to function, we become overwhelmed. Feeling overwhelmed simply indicates that we have too much going on in our heads.

Managing Feeling Overwhelmed

Step 1. Get the thoughts out of your head and write them down

Produce a list of everything that you must do or that is worrying you. Once your concerns are on paper, they each become a tangible item to tackle.

Step 2. Prioritise

Work through your list and decide what the most important things to deal with are. You cannot do everything at once. In this process, you will only address one thing at a time, so you must prioritise your list.

Don't get too hung up on the list itself. If anything needs changing, amend it later. You will likely have several minor things that are bothering you, but when you consider them against the others, you will find that they are low in priority. This process helps to eliminate this noise. Trust the process.

Step 3. Relax and smile for at least two minutes

Hang on! Ok, James, I was following Steps 1 and 2, but you've lost me at Step 3. What have I got to smile about? I know this sounds ludicrous, and it is probably the last thing you want to do, but there is science behind this approach. The physiological movement of smiling has a positive effect on the brain, even in the case of a fake smile. Try it now (but not on the train unless you want to freak your fellow commuters out).

When we smile, our bodies release chemicals called endorphins, which help us feel happier. So, smile and relax and take some deep breaths.

Step 4. Schedule the first thing on your list

In other words, decide when you will begin or complete your first task. The aim is to schedule it for today or tomorrow, at the latest.

Step 5. Take action

Taking action does not necessarily mean completing the full task at once, as a task might contain multiple layers, but you must move towards completion.

For example, perhaps you are worried about getting access to your children, and you don't know where to begin. A starting point could be to list the resources that can provide you with more information, such as the relevant chapter in this book, the Citizens Advice Bureau or a solicitor. Next, you would choose which action to complete first, for instance, reading the book chapter. By completing this task, you are taking a definitive step towards your overall goal.

Step 6. Celebrate

Every time you accomplish something, cross it off of your list and celebrate. Celebrating has a beneficial effect: it trains the mind. The mind likes to be rewarded, so celebrating every accomplishment teaches it to expect a reward after completing a task.

Soon, your mind begins to move in the direction of finding solutions to problems because it knows it will receive a reward. I know this concept sounds a bit strange, but science backs it up.

This process is simple, but it works. Aim to write your list each week. Writing will take longer at first, but once you have completed the exercise a few times, it will become second nature.

Allow yourself some downtime to take your mind off of your problems. Rather than going to the pub and waking up with a vicious hangover, find something else that you enjoy, especially if it involves other people. Perhaps this activity is something that you used to do but don't anymore or something new that you have always wanted to try.

Learn how to relax properly. A gruelling box-set session in front of the TV is not relaxing. Try deep breathing or meditation. Both have an incredible effect on your body. There are numerous meditation apps available, but I recommend *10 Percent Happier*, because it also explains how meditation works.

Make sure you are getting enough sleep. Go to bed at a time that allows you to get up early. Establish and maintain a routine. Win the morning, and you win the day.

Eat a balanced diet and make sure to exercise. We will cover this topic in a later chapter, but for now, remember: junk in, junk out. If you want to feel good and tackle anything that life throws at you, then fuel and train your body like the high-performance machine that it is. Exercise has the additional benefit of reducing stress instantly.

Finally, maintain a sense of humour. Laughter has been scientifically proven to really be the best medicine, so aim to see the humour in things. Chat with friends or watch stand-up or comedy shows. Not only will laughter make you feel better, but it has also been shown to boost your immune system.

Working out What Went Wrong

Separating can make you feel like a failure. Many people avoid the prospect of failure. In fact, we're so focused on not failing that we don't aim for success; instead, we settle for a life of mediocrity. As a result, we might ignore warning signs and gloss over the severity of the situation. To many people in our success-driven society, failure is seen as a kind of deficiency, a sign of intellectual inferiority. Many men would rather stay in a bad relationship to avoid being considered a failure. But let me tell you, real failure is staying in a loveless relationship. What would you rather do: spend 50 years in an unfulfilling relationship or admit that you messed up and then spend the next 50 years living a magnificent life?

In the tech and business world, there's a concept called "fail fast" that also applies here. Would you rather fail now and learn a lesson or take 50 years to learn that lesson, all the while dying slowly? The concept of failing fast isn't about failing for its own sake. Rather, the idea is to learn from your failures so that you can be happier, healthier and more fulfilled in the right relationship. The key is to learn from your mistakes.

Learning requires specific skills. It requires a positive attitude. It requires an open mind. It requires taking responsibility. So where do we begin? It's imperative that you first gain clarity on what went wrong. A review of the research highlights the seven primary reasons why couples separate:

1. Infidelity
2. Substance abuse
3. Lack of commitment
4. Too much conflict
5. Growing apart
6. Financial problems
7. Getting married too young

You also need to acknowledge and accept who instigated the separation. Was it you, was it your partner, or was it a mutual decision? If we take infidelity as an example, and you were the offender, you need to understand why you were unfaithful. Remember, the purpose isn't to beat yourself up. The goal is to learn from it so that it doesn't happen again.

Maybe you feel like you just can't stay with one woman. Well, that's fine, but don't enter into another serious relationship and make sure to be open and honest from the start. Maybe you got drunk, and you cheated. The lesson here is to know your limits and not put yourself in that situation again.

What if your ex-partner cheated on you? Remember, don't be a victim. Think about what you can learn from this instead. Is there some way that you could have contributed to the situation? Were you pushing her away? Was she just the wrong person for you? If so, what are the personality traits or the early warning signs that you can now recognise in future partners?

Lack of commitment, too much conflict, growing apart, and separating because you married too young all boil down to the same thing: conflicting values. What are values? Well, it's probably easier to begin with what values are not.

Values are not about which Netflix shows you like or what type of music you enjoy. Values are your personal, individual beliefs about what is most important to you. They represent your belief system about what is right and wrong, good and bad. We need values to move forward in life. Without them, we won't feel whole and fulfilled but, rather, empty. We feel personal satisfaction when our behaviour fulfils our values. This concept is called congruity.

Values govern our lives and how we respond to any given situation. They are like the human equivalent of iOS or Android. Every app, or experience, is affected by the operating system.

So where do our values come from? Values are specific, highly emotional beliefs that come from the environment we were raised in. Our mothers and fathers, our role models, tell us what to do and what not to do. We are rewarded if we accept their guidelines, and we are punished if we don't. Most of the values that we carry are programmed by this punish-reward technique. As we age, we also begin to internalise values from our teachers, friends and cultural icons such as sports and movie stars.

It is essential to understand our values so that we can choose the proper behaviours to support them. So how do we discover our values? We can ask ourselves a series of simple questions. For example, let's say that you want to find out what you value in an intimate relationship. You can begin by asking yourself: What is important to me in an intimate relationship, and why?

Let's say that love was your first answer. You would then ask yourself: What is important about love in a personal relationship? With each answer, ask the same question again until you feel that you have exhausted your list. Write your answers down on a piece of paper. You should have a list that looks like this:

- Love
- Happiness
- Compatibility
- Respect
- Openness
- Honesty
- Commitment
- Understanding
- Acceptance
- Appreciation
- Fun
- Beauty

Now that you have your list, you need to prioritise the entries. Using my example, start from the top and ask yourself if being happy is more important than being in love. Whichever takes priority gets the point. Work down the list, scoring each item against "love." When you've reached the bottom, start from the top again, this time scoring each item against the second value, "happiness."

After you complete the exercise, total up the scores for each value and rearrange the list from highest to lowest score. Once you have prioritised your most meaningful values, you can ensure that future relationships will align with these beliefs.

Although we are focusing on relationships, it is essential to recognise that the conflicts you have with your partner are not always about the relationship itself. A conflict arises when two people disagree with each other. A common source of disagreement in many relationships is money.

In this case, understanding your attitude and values around money can help you avoid discord in your relationship. Imagine, for example, that you believe in respecting money and using it wisely. If your partner doesn't appreciate money in the same way and prefers to spend it all, this disparity in values will create friction and tension within your relationship.

For this reason, it is essential to examine your values in several different aspects of your life. Quite often, people say that opposites attract. After all, contrasting personalities can certainly add intensity and excitement to a new relationship, and conflicts can generate sparks and sexual energy. However, the relationship will eventually sour.

If respect is important to you, but your partner tends to badmouth or belittle you, the disparity will create cracks in your relationship. Maybe honesty is vital to your partner, but you have a habit of telling little white lies. Or perhaps being adventurous is crucial to you, but your partner is more reserved.

Sometimes when we meet someone, the intensity of the relationship can obscure the difference in values. As the excitement settles down, cracks begin to form. You suddenly start to get annoyed by things that you never noticed before.

Our values are formed by various peer groups as we move through life. So as we grow older, our values and attributes can change. We sometimes find that we have less in common and don't want the same as our partner anymore. When we have different values from our partner, we might behave in a way that's incongruent with our own values, or we might impose our values on our partner. In either case, one or both parties may feel frustrated or conflicted.

The problem is that values are so deep-seated and carry so much emotion that they're hard to identify. We just feel some level of unease or discomfort. Sometimes, this small amount of pain can build over time and break the relationship. At other times, the pain is extremely powerful and causes immediate friction and conflict.

Now that you understand the importance of values, stop reading and complete the exercise described earlier. Go through each element of your life: your relationships, your career, your work, your attitude towards money, your attitude towards children. Ask yourself those questions and prioritise your values.

Once you have ranked your list, look through it to see if anything jumps out at you as a conflict that you had with your ex-partner. My problem arose once I had children and they became my number-one priority. After coming home from work, I would give all of my attention to my daughter. I didn't think I was doing anything wrong, and I felt that my ex-wife would understand my behaviour. However, I didn't realise that I was hurting her feelings. She no longer felt loved. Instead, she felt like she was second best.

I learned that I need to be more balanced and less extreme in relationships, which admittedly is difficult for me. I need to make sure that I make time for both my partner and my children, as they are both deserving of my love and attention.

The realisations that you gain from this process can be incredibly powerful. This process entails being accountable for your actions rather blaming somebody else. Identifying the part that I'd played in the breakup of my marriage and holding myself accountable made me feel good. It made me feel like I was acting in line with my values, that I was being responsible.

I felt so much better, because I knew that I'd discovered a valuable lesson. When you learn, you grow, and when you grow, you feel alive. Even though separation was not your life goal, you will become a better man if you learn from it.

Daily Gratitude Exercise

It is quite likely that you are not firing on all cylinders at the moment. You might feel down or find that your mood swings through emotions such as anger, regret and guilt. I want to give you a simple exercise that will help you feel considerably better about yourself and your future.

Holding on to negative thoughts can be extremely damaging to your health. This exercise is based on the principle that you cannot hold on to a negative emotion if you feel gratitude towards something else.

Depending on your current circumstances, finding things to be grateful for might be difficult, but if you stick with the process, I promise that you will feel better about yourself.

Get a pen and notebook for this exercise. For it to be effective, you must write down your answers. Just thinking about them in your head won't work, as your brain will merge together all of your other ideas, resulting in a vague notion at best. When you write a thought down, it becomes more real and tangible. It is no longer just a thought.

You can also use technology such as a phone, tablet or computer, but the physical act of writing is preferable because linking the mind and body unlocks our subconscious thoughts. Perform the exercise day and night for two weeks. If you keep up the practice, you will notice continued improvement in your mood and frame of mind.

Start each morning by completing the following:

1. Set a goal for the day.
   This is a goal that you will complete by the end of the day, so make sure it is achievable. It can be anything. Think about the day ahead and where you might be able to push yourself out of your current comfort zone. For example, you could say hello to five strangers, call a friend for a chat, go to the gym or eat healthily.

2. Decide what you are willing to give or do for others today.
   This is where reciprocity comes into play. Good things will happen to you when you give to others. So ask yourself: What am I willing to give to others today? It could be helping a colleague at work or merely acknowledging the homeless guy you pass every day on your way to work. Your good deed doesn't have to be major, but it must be something that you do for someone else.

3. Identify ten things that you are grateful for right now.

This intention might be hard at first, but stick with it. List ten things that you are grateful for: your health, your children, your parents, that the sun is shining, that you woke up this morning, that you have Wi-Fi! Keep going and make sure that you write down at least ten.

Getting into the habit of finding things that you feel grateful for is one of the best things you can do for yourself. This practice is about focusing on what is good in our lives and being thankful for the things we have. People who often feel grateful and appreciative are happier, less stressed and less depressed. Gratitude is an antidote to the sadness and disappointment we feel when we think about what is missing from our lives.

Positive emotions are contagious: one often leads to another. When we feel grateful, we might also feel happy, calm, joyful or loving.

Gratitude can also lead to positive actions. When we feel grateful for someone's kindness towards us, we are more likely to perform an act of kindness in return. In turn, our gratitude can have a positive effect on someone else's actions.

Don't just list big things. Recognising the small things is beneficial too, as they usually happen more frequently. One morning I found myself thinking about all of the people who enabled me to buy a cup of coffee: farmers, roasters, truck drivers, paper cup makers. It is incredible to consider everything that was involved in the process of making this seemingly minor thing we often take for granted.

4. Write one thing that you are grateful for that another person did for you.

Rather than a general feeling of appreciation, this habit seeks to identify precisely what it is about a person that you feel grateful for. Again, it doesn't have to be a grand gesture; a friend who simply makes you laugh works. Just make sure the act is recent and personal to you.

5. Write one thing that you are happy about right now.
    You might have to dig deep, but there will be something, somewhere that you can feel happy about. I love poached eggs, so eating poached eggs for breakfast makes me happy. Silly, perhaps, but what matters is that you find something. Even feeling only a glimmer of happiness indicates that the exercise is working. Stick with the task, and it will become more natural, more genuine and more powerful as you continue the process.

And that's it. The whole process shouldn't take longer than five or ten minutes. Finish it, then go about your day.

At the end of the day, come back to your notebook and complete the following three tasks:

1. Review your progress towards today's goal.
    Look at the goal that you set for the day and write a few words on how it went. Setting goals is very beneficial. There is the benefit of actually achieving your goals, of course, but the positives go deeper than that.

    Goals lead us to feeling hopeful and confident. They add a sense of structure and meaning to life. When we get into the habit of setting goals and striving to achieve them, we build our confidence to place even greater goals. Higher confidence in turn strengthens our resilience and develops a deep knowing that we can overcome the challenges that life throws at us.

2. Make a note of what you did or gave to others today.
    In the morning, you set yourself a goal to do or give something to another person. In the evening, write a few words about what you did and the outcome, especially how it made the other person feel and how it made you feel.

    Reviewing in this way reinforces constructive behaviour, because you feel great when you think about your good deeds. You are also being held accountable for that goal, so you are more likely to follow through on it.

3. Write down something that you are happy about.
    This could be something that happened to you or something that you did that you are celebrating. As you go through the process each day, you will find and document more and more good things that happened to you.

Record what happens over the next two weeks, and you will be amazed at how your feelings and your output will improve. You might want to give yourself a "happiness" score each morning to track your progress. There is no science behind it; just score how happy you feel on a scale of 1 to 10.

What you focus on is what you receive in life. If you pay attention to negativity, you will notice more and more things to feel negative about. On the other hand, if you direct your focus on positive things, you will experience more positivity. It really is that simple. If you want more of something, show appreciation for it, and it will naturally flow towards you.

Summary

The end of your relationship with your partner is going to be a painful, emotional period. Negative emotions are especially challenging to deal with, because we tend to avoid talking about them. In the same way that there is a stigma about mental health issues, there is a stigma around men talking about their feelings.

We are taught from a very early age to suppress our feelings and man up, but feelings are useful. They tell us that we need to deal with something to move forward in life. Working out what went wrong and how we contributed to it helps us make sense of our feelings. More importantly, doing so gives us focus and goals to strive for.

We only have 1440 minutes at our disposal every day. How we choose to spend this time will define the quality of our lives. If we decide to be mainly joyful, we will have a wonderful life. If we choose to stay angry, we will be miserable.

Research has shown that four minutes of anger suppresses our immune system for four hours. When we get angry with a person or situation, we are literally damaging ourselves. We reduce the effectiveness of our immune system and increase our risk of getting sick, all because of our anger.

The gratitude exercise is the perfect antidote for all negative and damaging emotions. Use it daily and train your mind to focus on the good in your life.

Our thoughts are the single most important factor in determining how we will behave and what we will achieve. Our thoughts determine how we feel, our feelings govern our actions, and our actions deliver the results. Life is what you make it, and we only get one shot at it. Choose to make it a good life.

CHAPTER 3.
COMMUNICATING WITH YOUR EX-PARTNER

It was November 2013, and I was attending an annual conference in Cannes on the French Riviera. I was sitting in a bar with a couple of friends, and the conversation came around to relationships.

Both men were divorced, and both had children. Mike and his ex-wife did not get on. They fought all the time, and he could not stand being anywhere near her. My other friend, John, asked Mike when he had last seen his daughter. Mike replied that he had not seen her in seven years.

In response to this, John inadvertently gave me one of the best pieces of advice of my life. John said that he always knew that he would not be able to maintain his relationship with his daughter if he didn't remain on good terms with his wife. Establishing a new type of relationship with his wife was the only way he could ensure that he would maintain contact with his daughter.

I was married at the time and had no intention of getting divorced, but those words resonated strongly and remained with me. This advice has become a cornerstone of my methodology. If you have children, you must try to establish and maintain a good relationship with their mother.

When you have children with someone, you can never totally separate from them. One way or another, you will feature in each other's lives. The decision to move on and establish a different type of relationship with your ex-partner is not easy. Unfortunately, some people find that they are never able to do so. If you go down this route, you will fill your own life, your ex-partner's life, and, even worse, your children's lives with unnecessary pain.

The previous chapter covered the inner game for good reason. You need to be match fit to deal effectively with the challenges ahead. From the very beginning, start with the end in mind. That way, when a situation arises, you are more likely to react in a way that will achieve your desired outcome rather than cause problems and have negative repercussions.

Written Communication

We have more ways than ever to communicate with each other, but this can be a double-edged sword.

Instant messaging is extremely useful, but it can be deadly in the wrong hands. It is too easy to fire off a message without fully considering how it could be perceived. Written communications can come across as too blunt or harsh. When we talk to someone in person, the recipient can hear our tone and see our body language. If a misunderstanding happens, we can quickly clarify our meaning. A poorly crafted message, on the other hand, can sometimes leap from the screen, and before we know it, we are in a frenzy typing an angry response. From now on, before you press send, reread your message at least once. If the topic is particularly sensitive, read it several times.

Avoid immediately responding to messages or emails. You might respond inappropriately or perhaps commit to something that you can't honour. However, if you have a habit of responding quickly but take too long to reply to a problematic message, your delay could be misinterpreted as ignoring the message. In this case, tell your ex-partner that you've received and read her message and will reply to her shortly. This way, you can take the time to write a properly thought-out response without her worrying that you're avoiding the discussion.

Good practice for this and all other parts of your life is to put your email and all of your messenger services into a folder on the second screen of your phone. Disable the badges (those little boxes with the numbers) and all notifications. This simple practice gives you control over your phone rather than your phone controlling you. Now you can respond to messages when you are ready rather than reacting to every notification.

Effective Communication

When couples separate, one or both may be upset or angry, which affects their ability to communicate. It is difficult to reach a favourable outcome regarding financial arrangements or access to children in this state of mind. Further, any angry exchanges will prolong the separation process, making it more painful and potentially costlier for everybody involved.

Poor communication is often a problem in our relationships, and it often continues to be an issue amongst separated couples. It is critical to communicate effectively, especially when dealing with your children's arrangements. But did you know that only seven percent of what we communicate is through words? Is it any wonder that we have trouble communicating sometimes? Thirty-eight percent of what we say is conveyed through the tone and volume of our voice, and fifty-five percent is expressed through our body language and facial expressions.

Facial expressions are a big giveaway, so it is essential to have control over your emotions and remain calm. Your words, gestures and facial expressions must match. If they don't, your ex-partner will sense that you are not being truthful. For example, you might say that you agree with something, but your tone and body language are communicating annoyance.

Preparation is the key. Before meeting, make sure you have your head in the right place by applying the techniques from Chapter 2 and using the following neutral, confident gestures:

- Spread your weight evenly across both feet whether standing or sitting
- Stand or sit up straight
- Relax your shoulders
- Keep your arms in an open posture
- Breathe slowly and deeply
- Speak slowly and clearly
- Use appropriate eye contact

The quickest way to control your mind is to manage your physical state. By applying these gestures, not only will you look confident, but you will also feel more confident, which will allow you to tackle difficult conversations more effectively.

Getting your point across and keeping the temperature down is not always easy. Fortunately, communication is not only talking; it's listening too. By learning to listen effectively, you can truly understand your ex-partner and discover her motivations.

Quite often, especially in a heated conversation, we don't listen to each other. We hear some of the words, fill in the gaps with assumptions and interrupt with our responses. Through active listening, we can be clear on what the other person is saying, which enables us to respond more effectively to get what we want.

Active listening requires us to concentrate on what is being said and to use clarification to better understand the meaning. For example, "What I think I'm hearing is… Is that right?" gives your ex-partner the opportunity to confirm that you have understood correctly or to clarify her position. This slows down the exchange and gives you a chance to respond rationally and reasonably, which helps to keep the temperature down.

Assertiveness

When we face a challenging conversation, it can sometimes be difficult to articulate our position calmly. For fear of losing control, we might decide not to raise a particular subject, or we might dance around it. The problem with this approach is that we are not clear about what we want, thus reducing our chance of getting it and creating more stress for ourselves.

We need to be assertive. When we are assertive, we can respond without blaming, attacking or withdrawing from the situation. Assertiveness starts with being clear on your rights and recognising and accepting that your ex-partner has rights that may be different from your own. In this way, we can get our point across calmly and confidently without being aggressive.

When we communicate, we have to take responsibility for our own feelings and opinions. No one else has the power to make you feel anything: not anger, not fear, not sadness, not even happiness. Emotions are our response to other people or to situations we find ourselves in. You can't always control a situation, but you can choose your response. When asserting your position, say, "I get frustrated when you talk to me like that" rather than, "You make me angry when you talk to me in that way."

Owning your feelings allows you to get your point across and encourages your ex-partner to respond, perhaps with a question to clarify the situation. The second statement, on the other hand, is likely to put her on the defensive and start the conversation on a downward spiral.

The words we use are incredibly powerful, and yet, we rarely give them more than our cursory attention. Delete "but" from your vocabulary. When a sentence contains "but," it minimises the importance of the preceding part. For example, "I'm sorry that I shouted at you, *but* you annoyed me" means if you hadn't annoyed me, I wouldn't have shouted at you.

We are all guilty of this, and the worst part is that we often say it when we don't even mean to disqualify the preceding statement; it's just a figure of speech. Rather than connecting the sentences using "but," use two separate sentences and make sure to pause between them. "I'm sorry I shouted at you. I got annoyed because of..." Now she hears your apology and the fact that you are annoyed, paving the way for constructive dialogue to resolve the situation.

Avoid using extreme statements, such as "You always..." and "You never..." Such statements are rarely true, and the conversation can reach an impasse over what is usually a throwaway comment. It would be more truthful and potentially more effective if you said, "The last two times you were late..."

If you are on the receiving end, calmly acknowledge the statement and present your perspective, emphasising the offending word. For example, "I'm not *always* late, although, admittedly, I was late on the last two occasions. I'm really sorry about that."

Objection Handling and Rehearsal

If you have a difficult or important conversation coming up, rehearse it. Write down what you want to say and then put yourself in your ex-partner's shoes. Write her likely responses, especially her objections. Follow with your responses to hers and work through each scenario until it reaches its logical conclusion.

This is a highly beneficial strategy, because it keeps surprises to a minimum. With practice, you can anticipate what she is likely to say with high levels of accuracy. Usually, when hit with an objection, our emotions rise while our intelligence falls. With rehearsal, we can prepare to handle objections and keep our emotions calm.

Here is a straightforward method for handling objections:

1. Acknowledge what has been said to demonstrate respect and that you are listening
2. Keep asking open questions until you get to the truth
3. Provide a closed-question solution
4. Get agreement

It works like this:

Her: "I'm not letting you see the children this weekend, because they are so naughty when they've been with you. You're a bad influence on them."
You: "Thank you for telling me about their behaviour." (Acknowledgment)
You: "In what way are they naughty?" (Open question)
Her: "Backchatting me, making a mess, not keeping their bedroom tidy."
You: "Do they ever backchat you at other times?" (Open question)
Her: "Well, yes, sometimes."
You: "Well, how about the next time I see them, I talk to them about being respectful and tidy when they get home. Would that work for you?" (Solution and closed question)
Her: "Yes, I suppose so." (Agreement)

The person who asks the question is always in control, so keep asking questions until you feel that you have determined the real root of the problem. After you ask a question, don't say anything until she responds. Don't attempt to fill the silence; keep quiet.

If she challenges you about asking questions, be open. Explain that you are asking questions because you are trying to get to the bottom of the problem. And if you can understand the problem, then you have a better chance of finding a solution.

Once you have your scripts down, run through them in your mind and feel the effect that the dialogue has on your body. Your brain doesn't know if what you are thinking is real or not. You can conjure the same physical responses by imagining something as you can by actually experiencing it.

Don't believe me? Consider this example. Have you ever been sick with worry? When we worry, we are thinking about something that hasn't happened; yet, we still experience the physical symptoms as if it were really happening. Rehearsal allows us to use that powerful effect to our advantage.

If you have privacy, take the rehearsal one step further and physically rehearse the interaction. Look into a mirror and say your script out loud using the right volume and tone of voice and with confident, open body language. By rehearsing the interaction and feeling the power of the words, you can desensitize yourself where appropriate to remain calm when the day comes.

Celebrate after each rehearsal. Play some uplifting music, jump around, pat yourself on the back and give yourself some positive self-talk. Be your own coach. Our minds love praise, and by providing our brains with what they want, we train them to automatically start rehearsing difficult situations until it becomes second nature.

To give your confidence a huge boost, try the following technique from Blair Singer, a coach of mine. It's called the Bragging Exercise. It only takes about 10 seconds, but it is extremely powerful.

You will need a quiet space away from other people, because you're going to look a little crazy doing this exercise. For this to work, you will have to be really loud, extremely animated and rather creative with the truth. In other words, you will have to make stuff up.

It works like this: get on your feet, beat your chest or stomp around – whatever it takes to create a massive burst of energy. Then, shout something like this:

"I AM SO CONFIDENT, I CAN HANDLE ANYTHING. GEORGE CLOONEY COMES TO ME FOR CONFIDENCE ADVICE. I AM SO CONFIDENT, I AM THE MOST CONFIDENT MAN IN THE WHOLE WORLD!"

It doesn't matter that this isn't true; it still has an incredible effect on your body and mind. Your adrenaline will be pumping and you will feel big, bigger than your physical body. Any doubts you had will be pushed to the side. Try it, don't hold yourself back and you will be amazed. To give your confidence a boost, do this exercise every day for two weeks.

Negotiation

At some point, you will have to negotiate with your ex-partner. Perhaps you will be negotiating the terms of the divorce, a financial settlement, or access to the children. Perhaps you will have to negotiate all three.

Some people think that negotiation is driving a hard bargain and getting your own way. This is one way; we call it Win-Lose. One person wins, one person loses. When you're negotiating a one-off transaction, such as buying a car, this is a perfectly acceptable negotiation tactic. After all, it doesn't matter if you upset the salesman; the most critical factor is getting the best price for the car. Negotiating a more complicated deal such as a divorce is an entirely different matter.

In the UK, the three elements of divorce are legally independent of each other. The problem with the Win-Lose approach is that the losing party will be dissatisfied when they lose and may attempt to recoup losses elsewhere in the negotiation. Even worse is that the frustration may rise to the point where your wife refuses to continue talking without the negotiating expertise of a solicitor.

A far better approach is Win-Win, where the parties work together to find an outcome that is suitable for both sides. In this approach, maintaining the relationship is essential, so the focus is on the outcome rather than personal disputes.

If you think that you could never be on friendly terms with your ex-partner, try to think of it as a business relationship instead. Now, think of a time you had business dealings with someone you disliked. Did you make the engagement easy for them? Of course you didn't; you were probably as disruptive as you thought you could get away with. This is human nature, and so it is between a couple who is separating.

If you dislike someone, you are likely to think only of your interests. You will push to achieve your objectives and fight even harder to protect your position. Even if you don't fight fire with fire, you will not make it easy for that person. You will not attempt to understand the other person to find the middle ground and to work out how you can both get what you want.

My recommendation is to find an affinity with your ex-partner. Clear your head of any malice, put the past behind you and seek to create a new type of relationship where you work effectively together to get what you both want. Now, I'm not suggesting that you roll over and give in to all of her demands, but listen, understand and consider what she has to say. Understanding is the basis of reaching the best possible agreement.

Always start the conversation with topics that you agree on. Establishing common ground gives you a platform to return to if things start to get heated. Agree on the agenda of each communication and stay on point.

Ask questions and never go first with your demands. Asking questions helps you understand the situation better. By understanding, you may find that you can secure a better outcome.

Negotiation can be difficult and takes time. Sometimes, you will hit an obstacle that appears impossible. When you do, know when to end the conversation. It's better to walk away and re-evaluate the situation than to provoke your ex-partner and cause her to entrench her position. Try to understand why she might be taking her position, and you might find a potential solution.

You will never get everything you want, but the chances are good that you will get more of what you want more quickly and at a much lower cost if you create rapport and communicate and negotiate effectively.

Dealing with Hostility

People are usually hostile for one of two reasons: to control a situation to get what they want, known as instrumental aggression; or as a reaction to something that has happened or that they perceive will happen to them, known as impulsive aggression.

Instrumental aggression is a learned behaviour that the practitioner has found to be a useful tactic to employ over the years. You probably already know if your ex-partner is prone to this method, because you will have been exposed to it before. If she does, you can now use this knowledge to your advantage and recognise that, for her, it is merely a means to an end.

Impulsive aggression signals that she feels that someone has wronged her in some way. This is helpful to understand, because if you are the source of the dissatisfaction, you can deal with it appropriately. If you are not the source, you can choose to distance yourself from it.

You are no longer responsible for your ex-partner's feelings. By all means, be empathetic if you want to, but don't get drawn in. Whereas once you might have shared and overcome emotional challenges together, now you are separate and responsible for your own lives. The only caveat is that if you do something to wrong her, then you need to take responsibility for your actions but not for her reactions. Whenever you do something wrong, apologise quickly. A genuine, heartfelt apology can work wonders.

How your ex-partner manages herself is up to her; however, if she sees you dealing with situations in a better way, she may learn from you. Don't try to teach or coach her, though. Let her come to you when and if she is ready.

When emotions are high, the part of the brain responsible for reasoned judgement is switched off. So when faced with high levels of anger, recognise that your ex-partner has lost temporary control. She is unable to think calmly and rationally. You are no longer communicating with a person; you are confronted by the raw emotion of anger. There is no point in trying to reason with anger; it just won't listen. Instead, let it get everything out and actively listen.

Once she has finished, summarise what you think you have heard and let her correct you where necessary. Once you have a clear understanding, you can decide what you can or cannot do about it. A great strategy is to ask her what her ideal solution is. Once you know what she wants and you know what you are willing to do, you can start to negotiate a perfect outcome for both of you.

If you find yourself getting angry in response, count to 10! I know this is age-old advice, but the real point is to pause and take stock of the situation rather than merely react. Ask yourself:

- Why am I engaging in this argument?
- What do I want to achieve from it?
- How am I going to do that?
- How likely will I achieve my goal?
- What are the risks?

Once you have evaluated your position, you can proceed with the best option. You might need to argue your point on this occasion. Alternatively, you might choose to back down and live to fight another day. In this case, divert the argument by saying, "We don't seem to agree at the moment. Let's park this for now and talk about..."

Recognise the feeling of anger in your body and quickly

check your body. Again, the quickest way to control your mind is to change your physical state. If you are angry, your body is probably tense. Consciously relax your body, unclench your firsts, unfold your arms and drop your shoulders. Relax your jaw, slow your breathing and breathe deeply from the stomach. Control your voice, keep your tone level and speak slowly at an average volume. By controlling your body, you will control your mind and respond more appropriately.

Don't react to personal remarks, insults or aggression. Recognise that your ex-partner is struggling to manage her anger. If a remark is particularly hurtful, address it at a later date when you are both calm. A useful tool is the "When you..., I feel..." model.

This model is a two-part communication tool to help you clearly express your feelings when they are related to another person's behaviour. For example, "When you shout at me in that way, I feel embarrassed, as I don't want our neighbours and friends to hear us argue like that."

Old grievances can also be a regular source of conflict. If this is a problem for you, agree on an agenda with your ex-partner before each discussion, and bring it back on track if you start to deviate to old issues.

If it is a new and valid issue, acknowledge it, but ask that you discuss it after you have covered all of the other points. Not only does this establish the process by which you will communicate, it also allows time for the new situation to abate, resulting in a calmer discussion.

Summary

Remember, the objective is to reduce conflict and communicate effectively and respectfully. If the relationship is currently fractious, operate within a communication framework. Set an agenda, stay on topic and discuss one problem at a time. An excellent technique to lower the temperature is to first address the things you are likely to agree on before delving into more sensitive areas.

Avoid finger-pointing. If your relationship is over, it's over. There is no point in either of you wasting energy trying to score points. If you are prone to this, set boundaries before you start the conversation. Explain that you want to focus on finding solutions collaboratively. If you find yourselves getting into the blame game, bring the discussion back to the agenda.

Be willing to compromise and be flexible, but don't give everything away. Make sure that you know where your boundaries are and where you can compromise. Be creative. Remember, the better the plan before the conversation, the more likely you will get a favourable outcome. If you're uncertain about something and need more information or time to think, then say so. Don't be afraid to do this rather than risk committing to something that you cannot do. Being a man of your word builds trust.

One final point: try not to argue with your ex-partner in front of your children. Your children love both of you. It is stressful for them to hear the two people they love most arguing with each other. Conversations such as access arrangements and your financial agreements are for adults only. Avoid dumping this pressure on the children. Even if they are engrossed in something else, don't assume that they are not listening. If they are within earshot, they are undoubtably listening.

CHAPTER 4:
CONNECTING WITH YOUR CHILDREN

The initial period of separation is probably the worst time in a father's life. In 90% of cases, the children remain with their mother, and she becomes the resident parent. The father becomes the non-resident parent and suddenly finds that someone else now has control over the time he can spend with his children.

Couples separate for a reason, and in the early days, there will be tension. It is a sad fact that a common practice is for the mother to deliberately restrict a father's access to his children in the early stages, which can go on for some months.

There are several reasons why this happens, and you might be experiencing it right now. I wish I could share with you a hack to resolve this situation, but the reality is that there is little you can do about it in the immediate term. In the UK, the law is stacked against the parent who doesn't reside with the children.

While there is not much you can do to achieve a positive outcome, there is a great deal you can do to cement a negative one. Damage limitation is the objective. Proceed with caution, keep calm and play the long game. Don't do anything that can be held against you in the future. Don't shout and avoid arguments with your ex-partner.

Whatever you do, don't abuse (verbally or physically) or hurt your ex-partner or anybody else involved. Keep a precise record of everything that happens. I know this is frustrating, and you will find yourself questioning why you must do it, but your records will prove especially useful if you must escalate the issue to higher powers.

Do not try and take your children from school or anywhere else without consent from the mother. Be patient, and when you do see your children (which you will), calmly explain the situation to them. Tell them that you want to see them and that you are trying to resolve some problems with their mum. Let them know that you are there and that the situation will be worked out soon.

Keeping in touch with your children is much easier when they are older and have mobile phones and email accounts, but it is particularly challenging with young children. The best you can do is to know that the situation will pass and to keep calm and controlled.

The first step in overcoming any challenge is to have an awareness of the situation. Therefore, you must recognise that your role as a father has changed. Living together in the family home is a considerably different dynamic to your new reality. As soon as you moved out of the family residence, your role automatically changed. Most of the responsibilities and activities of being a parent now fall on the adult who maintained the residency.

From now on, as a non-resident father, activities such as school runs and mealtimes will no longer happen or will occur on a reduced basis. I found this particularly challenging. I was lucky enough to be able to spend a lot of time with my children, and I always made sure that I was there for at least one meal each day. Whenever possible, I took my daughter to school and would be home to read a bedtime story.

On the face of it, there is nothing unique or special about such things, but when they are taken away from you, and you realise that you will never have them again, it's a real blow to the stomach. For many fathers, it feels like fatherhood has been taken away from them. Of course, this is not the case, as there is more to being a parent, but it hurts like hell nonetheless.

You need to come to terms with your new reality and realise that this is your new life, and this is how it's going to be from now on. Focus on what you can do and how you can be a positive influence in your children's lives rather than wasting your energy on what you cannot control.

Focusing on the negatives, on your frustrations or injustice, will only make you angry and bitter. It will increase your stress levels. It will prolong the pain. No one in this world can make you feel unhappy except for you, and the opposite is also true.

We create our own emotions based on the meaning we give to a situation.

Now, I'm not suggesting that you climb into a happy bubble and let any bad event wash over you. What I am suggesting is that you control the effect any situation has on your wellbeing. Do you want to live a long and healthy life? Of course you do. So, don't let someone else damage your health by allowing their actions to have total control over your body's response.

Focus on what you can do. It is essential that your child understands that you are there for them and that they are your number-one priority; in other words, that you are still their dad. You need to know what is going on in your child's life, which means taking an interest in their school, class work, extracurricular activities, sports and activities and friendships. Even things that you once may have taken for granted, such as favourite TV shows, pop stars and the latest toys and gadgets, provide opportunities to understand your child and form deeper bonds.

Recognise that separation is not all doom and gloom. In fact, it's an opportunity to be an even better dad than you were before. Many fathers get home from work exhausted and crash in front of the TV, spending very little quality time with their children. In many cases, it is not their fault: our society has us working ever longer hours, and we are increasingly stressed due to a poor work-life balance.

Now you have an opportunity to decide what kind of father you will be, to determine how you will contribute to your child's life and how you will be a positive influence. Look at your situation from this perspective, and you might find that you have been handed a blessing. After all, what is more important than your children? Isn't it better to suffer the pain of a breakup but be an outstanding father than to look back from your deathbed wishing you had done more? If only one good thing comes from your divorce, make sure it is that you are an outstanding father who positively influences his children's lives.

The Parenting Plan

You can use a parenting plan to help shape the father you want to be. A parenting plan is a voluntary agreement between a child's parents. Most child agencies around the world have one, but it is simply a document that describes how you and your ex-partner will raise your child. You can find a copy in the Appendix or download a free version at www.realmansdivorce.com.

A parenting plan is not as unusual as it sounds. You most likely had a parenting plan when you were with your partner, but it just wasn't written down. You and your partner probably established rules for things like mealtimes, bedtimes and how much TV your children could watch. These rules and expectations constituted your parenting plan.

Now that you are separated, you need to talk with your partner to agree on how you will bring up your children. The parenting plan provides the framework for this conversation. A coherent plan will help reduce misunderstandings and conflict and provide everyone involved with clear boundaries.

If your relationship is particularly strained, approach this arrangement as a business partnership, where your business is raising your children in the best possible way. In this context, a parenting plan is somewhat like a business plan, as it describes how you will manage your business.

The parenting plan starts by detailing when both parents will have access to their children. This can be a difficult topic and a source of conflict, especially in the short term. However, the parenting plan is medium to long term; it is where we want to get to. Remember, always begin with the end in mind.

You need to think about when and how often you will see your children. Understandably, you will want to see them as much as possible, but this will be dependent on several factors.

Will you see them on weekends only, or can you see them on some weeknights as well? How long will you see them for? During the day or overnight too? Consider what you will do with them when you are with them. Think about what help or what resources you will need to establish the contact. Don't forget about other relationships, such as with grandparents. Grandparents will miss your children too, so consider how often you can facilitate those visits.

How will the school holidays be split between parents? Can you divide all of the school holidays between you and their mum, or do you need to organise childcare? Can you both take the children out of the country at holiday time?

Think about your plan for special events, such as birthdays and Christmas. Will you alternate or both attend? The children would be delighted if both parents were present on Christmas Day, but this can sometimes be difficult. So, what will you do? Will you visit during the day? And how will you decide who buys which presents?

If you have young children, agree on who will buy presents for other special days such as Mother's Day or Father's Day. Will you do it or will the grandparents?

Some elements of the plan will depend on your child's age. If they are young, they are unlikely to have their own phone. The frequency of contact via phone or video messaging will greatly depend on the current state of your relationship with their mother. If you are on good terms, communication is likely to be more regular and flexible. But if the relationship is strained, you might have to schedule specific times during the week.

The next section describes house rules in each home. Many rules will be the same for both parents, but it is okay if they are different as long as there are clear boundaries and the differing rules don't negatively affect the other parent. For example, it would be unreasonable to regularly allow your child to stay up past 10pm over the weekend if their bedtime is usually 7pm and if the late nights make them tired for school.

Children love routine, so consider the various elements of their day and decide whether they need to be included in the plan. What time do they wake up? What do they have for breakfast? Will you have rules about eating certain foods before treats or staying at the table until everyone is finished? When should homework be done? What other tasks or jobs do they have? How much screen time can they have? How will you discipline the children?

Discuss internet and social media access. Will you let them go on YouTube or Facebook? Up to what age classification of films can they watch? What computer games can they play? Can they play with their friends outside? What time do they have to be home?

How can you both be involved in your children's education? What arrangements will you make for parents' evening, school plays and sports days? How will you discuss and agree on choices around school, college and university?

The parenting plan also describes how you and your ex-partner will communicate with one another. Will it be via phone? Text? Messaging service, such as WhatsApp or email? Are there inappropriate times to contact each other? What is the procedure in an emergency?

How will you manage disagreements between the two of you? What decisions, if any, must you take jointly? How much notice do you need for a change in any of the arrangements? What happens if one of you dies? Checking out is obviously not on your to-do list, but every 22 minutes, a parent with dependent children dies in the UK.

We provide support for our children, usually with monthly payments from our earnings, but what happens if we die? Who will support them then? Take out a life insurance policy so that your children will still be supported if you die. It provides peace of mind, and it does not have to cost a lot of money.

Don't be a perfectionist and assume that you must reach an agreement on every aspect of the plan for it to be worthwhile. Start with the essentials and secure your time with your children. Further arrangements will develop over time as you and their mum adjust to the dynamics of your new partnership.

Access to Your Children

Since I travelled regularly for work, it was critical for me to secure contact with my children so that I could fit everything else around those dates. I ensured that my children knew when they would see me and that I knew when I would see them. This enabled me to deal with all the additional complications, such as the logistics of travelling there, booking accommodations and planning activities that I would do with them.

In the early stages, it is advisable to book flexible tickets and be prepared for changes. However, as time passes and you develop a better working relationship with your ex-partner, the situation will settle down, and the parenting plan will come into play.

Before you begin any conversation about the parenting plan, consider what you want so that you can determine your range of negotiation. For example, one of the first things to think about is when and for how long you will see your children.

The idea is to see them as much as possible, but work and other life commitments might get in the way. Their mum will also want to spend time with the children, so the two of you need to negotiate how much time you will each have with them. Your range will include the maximum amount of time you are able to spend with your children and the minimum that you are willing to accept. Having set your range, you now know what an acceptable deal looks like and, more importantly, what a no-deal looks like.

The age of the children can have an impact on this proposal. It is more straightforward when your children are young, but as they get older and they have their own commitments with friends or clubs, it is understandable that time with you might sometimes clash with their plans. Making the best of any agenda conflicts will require your understanding, flexibility and creativity.

In the early stages, my advice is to place your focus on your child's needs. Yes, you are the one going through the separation, and the pain might be unbearable, but remember that however hard it is for you, it is likely ten times harder for your children. As time goes by, you need to find balance in your life by creating time for yourself as well as for your children. But in the early stages, put your children first and make sure that they are getting what they need from you during this difficult time.

The best scenario you can hope for is your ex-partner wanting you to have as much access as possible to your children. Research consistently shows that shared parenting relieves the emotional loss children feel when parents separate. It helps to reduce poverty, minimises anti-social behaviour and improves health, education and work performance. It also provides a solid foundation for the children's own family relationships later in life.

While the non-resident parent suddenly has a greater capacity for building their social life, the resident parent has probably taken on even more responsibility. Presumably, your ex-partner wants to get on with her own life as well, so she should be keen for you to have access to facilitate this desire.

This scenario is a great place to be in, but make sure that you are not being manipulated and that it works for you and, more importantly, for the children. Remember, you are not a babysitting service. However, if it works for you, and if it means increased contact particularly in the early stages, do it. Just make sure that you come back to a plan that is achievable in the long term and that has a flexible element to it.

Flexible means the ability to have additional days to see the children if the opportunity arises and for your partner to ask you to take care of the children if she has some unplanned engagements.

With all the best intentions in the world, there will be times when you can't keep to the parenting plan or accommodate an additional request. If a specific day doesn't work, offer alternatives to make up the time. Doing so will reinforce the collaborative environment necessary for successful co-parenting.

So how much time should you spend with your children? I've seen formulas that calculate ideal time to spend together based on the age of the children. Quite frankly, this approach is ridiculous.

Some propose only seeing children for a couple of hours a week with no opportunity for them to stay overnight with the father. How can you develop or maintain a relationship with your child with so little contact? All successful relationships require regular contact, and the one with your child is no exception.

Everyone's circumstances are different, but I'll share with you my situation and what I did. My children are 300 miles away from me, which is a five- to six-hour drive each way. I wanted to make sure that I was able, in the limited time frame that I had, to maintain a high level of normality around things like mealtimes and bedtime routines.

To achieve this, I created an environment where the children could stay over with me. In the beginning, my daughter was four, and my son hadn't even reached his first birthday. Therefore, it was incredibly important to me to raise my children like I would if I was the resident parent. When we all lived together, I took an active role in raising them, so I wasn't going to stop now. Of course, it is challenging when you are on your own and no longer in the same home, but you just have to be more organised, such as when you take the children on holiday.

If your children are very young, don't presume that you won't be able to cope with a situation like this and thus shy away from it. You can do it, and you will find that you will soon get to grips with it. You will never get this time with your children again, so don't lose it.

The bitter truth is that no matter how much time you spend with your children, it may never feel like enough after the many years you'd spent living under the same roof. You might be wracked with guilt, but you must overcome.

Realise that the objective is now quality, not quantity. Really focus on your children, and when you are with them, devote all of your time and attention on them.

When you all lived together, work, chores and life prevented you from devoting 100% of your attention to your children. Now you are free from this. Now you can focus on them and enjoy quality time together. Just think about that for a minute: How often and for how long did you place 100% of your attention on your children when you lived together? Now calculate how much time you have to do so now. You are likely to find that the amount of quality time exceeds that when you lived together.

If you want to be a role model and have an influence, you must be present and maintain a minimum level of involvement. While indirect contact through phone calls, emails and video conferencing such as FaceTime and WhatsApp are a huge help, they are no replacement for in-person contact.

Understandably, your ex-partner will be concerned about the children's safety and whether their needs will be met. You will need to talk with her and put her mind at rest, especially if you want overnight access. You must ensure that your accommodations are suitable. Your children will already feel sensitive, so you don't want to take them somewhere grim and miserable. Create an environment that feels normal and won't worry them. In the early stages, you might have to rely on a family member, such as a grandparents' house, if money is in short supply.

Spending Time with Your Children

So, what do you do with your children once you are with them? First and foremost, your children want to see you and spend time with you. When you haven't seen them in a while, you might be tempted to go all-out and plan a weekend of exhausting activities. I was definitely guilty of this.

The thought of keeping the children in a boring hotel room all weekend was a huge driver behind my agenda. However, over time, I realised that my children enjoyed simple and less strenuous activities too: watching a movie, doing arts and crafts and playing board games. I found that we were able to engage more deeply during these low-energy activities.

There is no single best use of your time with your children. However, I urge you to make sure that you spend the time attentive to your children. We are bombarded by so many distractions these days, especially from that supercomputer in our pocket.

Avoid being one of those parents who ignore their children and is always glued to their phone.

Remember, you are a role model. Mobile phone use is an epidemic. It enslaves and damages us and our children. Be the one who isn't on the phone; your children will thank you for it now and when they're older. When I'm with my children, I don't even switch my work phone on until they have gone to bed. When I'm with them, work waits. That is a line that I don't cross.

It is essential to make sure that you take your children shopping for presents for their mum and grandparents. She is their mum, and it's crucial that they understand the importance of thanking their mother. Even if the mother doesn't reciprocate, you know what's right, so do the right thing.

Talk to your children to understand what is going on in their lives. Find out what they are learning at school, what they enjoy and don't enjoy and who their friends are. Keep a note of what they have told you in previous conversations so that you can keep track of their progress.

Look for ways to nurture their interests. If they are learning about volcanoes, think of ways to bring this lesson to life through simple home experiments or visits to a museum or exhibition. If they show interest in a sport, practice with them or take them to a trial or live event. I believe we can do anything if we put our minds to it, so one of my jobs as a father is to make sure my children are aware of all the opportunities that life offers.

If you find activities that you both enjoy, you will further strengthen your relationship. Choose activities that encourage communication, as they will help you identify and understand your child's strengths and weaknesses. In turn, you will have the opportunity to teach your child, and you will both develop a deep sense of caring and respect for each other.

By tapping into the seeds of interest, you might help your child find their lifelong passion. What could be better? Get their feedback to make sure that you are doing activities that they enjoy and find stimulating.

The activities don't have to be expensive. Children love to be outdoors, so plan treasure hunts or go hiking, running or cycling. Camping provides plenty of opportunities to do things they may not usually do at home, such as cooking, washing up or fetching water. Helping out in this way gives children a sense of responsibility and autonomy.

Arts and crafts, puzzles, board games, rolling skating and even video games in moderation give you the opportunity to work together as a team or play competitively. These games also give you the chance to understand each other, get in the zone, have a lot of fun and truly nurture a relationship that sets them up for life.

Nurturing a Relationship with Your Children

You must be approachable to your children. Create a safe zone and don't judge. If your child comes to you with a thought or a question, nurture it. You want your child to be curious and to learn to think for herself.

Even if they have done something wrong and come to you, don't get angry. By choosing to confide in you, they are asking for your help. It doesn't mean you condone what your child has done, but we all make mistakes, so help them find a solution.

You must keep your children as close to you as possible, because if you push them away, there are plenty of other people and things that will draw them in. Always give them a way back; never close the door on them.

Let your child know that you love them. Now, I'm a British man, so the most affection I show with my own parents is a firm handshake. But all joking aside, life is different now. Being nurturing is no longer just the preserve of mum. When you are with your children, you need to provide emotional support too. Tell them that you love them, be affectionate and be thoughtful.

I take a mini printer with me when my children and I go out and do activities so that I can take photos with my phone and print the pictures on the go. I also write letters from time to time. I have special paper and envelopes, and I write them a letter and include a picture as well. It doesn't have to be *War and Peace*, just a few sentences. It's so uncommon but so nice to get a handwritten letter these days, and children really love it.

Be there for sports events and school plays. Children greatly appreciate both parents being there, so go together if you can.

Volunteer to help out with school activities. Usually, this is something that mums tend to do. But from experience, let me tell you that not only is this rewarding for you, you will also see first-hand how important it is for your children. They love telling their friends about their dad, so remember that you are a leader and you are there to inspire.

My daughter was feeling nervous about starting a new school. I remembered a wonderful quote from Roald Dahl: "If you have good thoughts they will shine out of your face like sunbeams and you will always look lovely." I told her this quote a few times and wrote it in a card I sent to her before the big day. She went to school all smiles and full of confidence and had a brilliant day.

Congratulate them on their success and teach them the importance of determination, persistence and having a flexible approach.

Maintaining Family Traditions

Carving pumpkins for Halloween, wearing silly Christmas jumpers and singing carols: traditions play an important part in children's lives. They can be very meaningful and are often the childhood memories that children remember as adults and carry on with their children.

Maintain and split the traditions if you must. For example, if your weekend doesn't fall on Halloween, carve the pumpkins on the nearest weekend and find a party to attend.

Spend Christmas together if you can or alternate Christmas with your children. Potentially even better for your children is to have two Christmases! One on Christmas day and another one on Boxing Day.

Don't forget the little things too. Bath time and story time were important in my household, and I try to maintain them to this day.

Make a note of all the little things that you did with your children and try to preserve them. Being separated also gives you the opportunity to create new traditions together, so actively seek out inspiration.

Discipline

Discipline is how we provide guidance to our children and teach them how to behave. Our children copy what we do, so always lead by example. Aim to have a consistent approach to discipline with their mother. Children learn to play one parent against the other, particularly after separation. The parenting plan helps you achieve some consistency; the more consistency there is, the easier it will be to teach your child how to behave appropriately.

There are two types of consistency with discipline. There is consistency between parents, which you will agree through the parenting plan, and there is consistency in terms of how you deliver the discipline.

If you are stressed, then the consistency of discipline may change. You might become less tolerant and lose your temper, or you might totally ignore the behaviour, both of which are confusing for the child.

When you only see your children on the weekend, you may not want to discipline them. However, rules are necessary. If they test you with, "My mum lets me do that," just tell them, "When you are with me, this is the rule."

All children are going to test limits. That's how they learn about the world. Following separation, children are likely to do this more frequently because of the reduced communication between the parents. And they are likely to be more successful. You might hear your child say, "But mum lets me stay up until 9pm," or, "I always watch the iPad before bed." The first step is to recognise that they're doing it. Laugh it off, and tell them that you know what they are trying to do.

Even if it is something that their mum lets them do but not something you allow, again, tell them, "Look, that's fine, but when you're with me, that's the rule." My son loved milk before bedtime, but it had to stop when he was being nappy trained. For months, I hadn't given him any, and he rarely asked for it. Then one day, I was picking him up from his mum when she asked if I wanted a beaker for his milk, to which my son replied with a cheeky grin, "Daddy doesn't let me drink milk when I'm with him"!

Children understand that there are different rules in different households, and they can manage that. If you and their mum are aligned on the fundamentals, it is okay to have differences on minor rules.

Summary

Securing regular, uninhibited access to your children can be one of the biggest challenges that you will face during separation. Raising children is hard work too, especially as a single parent. You might find yourself thinking: Is it worth it? Would they be better off without me?

Don't allow negative self-talk or negative comments from others to take residence in your mind. Never lose sight that children are the most important thing in the world. My message to you is never give up hope, and never give in.

Do not let the opportunity to be an amazing father evade you, no matter what pressure you are currently under. You will get through it.

One day you will look back, and you won't feel the pain anymore. We humans are incredible beings: we forget the hardships and remember only the successes. This tendency is what keeps us alive and pushes us forward.

Divorce and separation are no different. You will forget the pain, and all you will be left with from that period are memories of the happy times with your children.

Your relationship with your children is the result of the time and energy you spend with them. You don't have to be a child psychologist to be a good dad. You simply need to be present and provide guidance, encouragement, love and words of wisdom.

CHAPTER 5:
HANDLING THE LEGAL PROCESS OF DIVORCE

One of the only things I was sure of when my wife and I first separated was that I wanted to keep my legal costs as low as possible. Having worked with many lawyers in both my professional and personal life, I knew that when faced with a challenge, there is nothing better than having a good lawyer by your side. However, that expertise comes with a very hefty price tag.

A partner or legal director of a large corporate firm charges over £400 per hour. Even a trainee bills more than £100 per hour. Then, of course, the VAT is added on top of that.

I had heard stories of divorcing couples who had racked up legal costs in the tens of thousands. They weren't millionaires; they were ordinary people like you and me. This just seemed insane to me. Why on earth would anyone want to line the pockets of a law firm when that money could be put to good use elsewhere? The answer is simple: legal costs are in direct proportion to conflict.

The very nature of divorce implies some form of conflict; otherwise, you would stay together. Likewise, the premise of our legal system is that someone will win. What we think of as a way to resolve conflict can, in fact, fuel and prolong it.

The good news is that you can avoid this issue. With planning, you can keep your legal costs as low as possible. First and foremost, when you meet with solicitors, find out exactly what their costs are likely to be. Do not feel embarrassed to ask about money. A solicitor's number-one objective is to make money for their firm by providing a service. All law firms record and bill for the time of their employees, and all of the large firms set individual annual targets. Some solicitors will offer a fixed price. Others will bill in minutes or hours.

Get recommendations where possible and speak to several solicitors to find out how they would approach your situation.

Their approach and personality need to match your strategy. It's no good to hire a super aggressive solicitor if you plan to reach a mutually acceptable compromise with your wife.

Ask the solicitor how long they think it will take to resolve your situation, and get an estimate of the cost. It is critical to understand the costs and the time the whole process will take in order to avoid any nasty surprises. Remember, whatever estimate they give you is likely to be at the low end of the range.

There will be additional costs for administrative tasks such as printing and photocopying, so make sure you receive a complete list of charges and ask them for the total estimated price based on your situation.

There are three elements to consider when divorcing:

1. The legal divorce: I recommend that you complete this mostly yourself, as it is straightforward.
2. The division of property and money: I recommend that you try and agree on this with your wife first but use a solicitor to write up the settlement plan to submit to the court for approval.
3. The child arrangements: I recommend that you agree informally with your spouse to avoid the legal process altogether, because this step is costly and inefficient.

If you can land these three recommendations, your legal costs will be greatly reduced. You might also find that the relationship with your ex-wife will be more harmonious, because you were focused on finding solutions and reaching an agreement rather than fighting for your position. Every time you fight, you are likely to entrench her position. And every time you fight and a solicitor is involved, more of your hard-earned cash will eventually find its way into the solicitor's bank account.

Set out from the start to keep your legal costs as low as possible. Beginning with the end in mind will help you make the right decisions and hopefully avoid unnecessary and costly arguments. Tell your solicitor that this is your objective; a good lawyer will respect this and advise you if you start to deviate from your plan.

In whatever capacity you choose to employ a solicitor, make sure that you maximise the time that you have with them. Prepare for the meetings in advance, making sure to list all the points that you want to discuss and any details you want to share. Their time is valuable, so you don't want to leave a meeting only to find that you have missed something that you wanted to discuss. Do not use your solicitor to vent your frustration. They are simply there for legal advice. Use your friends and other networks for emotional support. This approach will be much cheaper.

In the meeting, take notes and summarise the key points and the next actions. Provide any additional documents the solicitor requests as soon as possible. Agree with the solicitor on who will be responsible for which parts of the proceedings.

The divorce itself is quite straightforward; we will examine the steps in the next section. If you can reach a financial agreement with your spouse, you can save money by appointing a lawyer to manage the financial consent on an execution-only basis. Coming to an agreement about finances will depend on the complexity of your potential situation, the relationship you have with your wife and the amount of time that you are able to devote to the process.

It is essential that the financial consent order provides a clean break, which means that once the assets and liabilities have been appointed, neither party can try to add or take away something at a later date.

Getting a Divorce in England and Wales

To start divorce proceedings in England and Wales, you must satisfy the following conditions:

- You must have been married for one year.
- Your permanent home must be in England or Wales, or you are domiciled in these countries if you live abroad.

You or your wife can apply for the divorce. It does not matter who files for divorce; however, the petitioner, the person who files, must pay the £550 court fee. It is possible to reduce this cost if the petitioner receives certain benefits or is under a certain income threshold. If these criteria apply to your wife, it may be more beneficial for her to file, if you both agree to the divorce.

The steps that follow assume that you are filing the divorce. If your wife files, the process is the same except that you become the respondent.

Step 1. Grounds for Divorce

When you apply for a divorce, you must prove that your marriage has broken down by selecting one or more of the following five reasons:

- Adultery – Your spouse has had sexual intercourse with another person of the opposite sex.
- Unreasonable behaviour – Your spouse has behaved in such a way that you cannot reasonably be expected to live with them, such as physical or verbal abuse, lack of sex, financial recklessness or a lack of socialising.
- Desertion – Your spouse has deserted you for a continuous period of more than two years.
- Separated for two years with consent – You both agree to the divorce.
- Separated for five years with no consent – You do not need your spouse's agreement.

You can be separated while living in the same home if you're no longer together as a couple (for example, if you sleep and eat apart). If your wife agrees to the divorce, you can easily file the divorce yourself. If she doesn't, and she is likely to contest it, you will need the assistance of a solicitor.

Step 2. Filing for Divorce

To apply for the divorce yourself, go to https://www.gov.uk/apply-for-divorce. You can either download the *D8 Application* form and apply by post or follow the steps to apply online.

Before you apply for a divorce, you will need your wife's full name and address and your original marriage certificate or a certified copy. Once you have completed the application, pay the £550 court fee so that the court can begin to process the application.

If you are applying by post, you need to send three copies of the D8 form (four copies if you name someone your wife committed adultery with) to your nearest divorce centre. Your nearest divorce centre can be found by following the instructions at https://courttribunalfinder.service.gov.uk.

The court will review your application once they have received it. If all of the information is correct, you will be sent:

- A notice that your application has been issued.
- A copy of your application stamped by the divorce centre.
- A case number.

Your wife will be sent a copy of your application and an acknowledgement of service form, which asks if she intends to defend the divorce. She must respond within eight days. If you named the person your wife committed adultery with, they will also be sent a copy of the application and be asked to respond.

Step 3. Apply for a Decree Nisi

You can apply for a decree nisi if your wife does not defend your divorce petition. A decree nisi is a document that states that the court does not see any reason why you cannot divorce. You can still apply for a decree nisi if your wife does not agree to the divorce, but you will have to go to a court hearing to discuss the case, where a judge will decide whether to grant you the decree.

To apply for the decree nisi, complete the *D84 Application for a Decree Nisi* form. You must also complete one of five *D80 Statement in Support of Divorce* forms. Both documents are very straightforward. You select the D80 form based on one of the five reasons given for your divorce:

- Adultery statement.
- Unreasonable behaviour statement.
- Desertion statement.
- Two years' separation statement.
- Five years' separation statement.

Once completed, send the documents, along with a copy of your wife's response to the divorce petition, back to the court.

If the judge agrees, the court will send you and your wife a certificate, which will tell you the time and date you will be granted a decree nisi. Once received, you must wait 43 days (six weeks and one day) before you can apply for a decree absolute to end the marriage.

Step 4. Apply for the Decree Absolute

The decree absolute is the legal document that ends your marriage. You need to apply within 12 months of receiving the decree nisi; otherwise, you will have to explain the delay to the court.

To apply for a decree absolute, complete the *D36 Application for Decree Nisi to be made Absolute* form. The courts will check that the time limits have been met and that there are no other reasons not to grant a divorce. The court will then send you and your ex-partner a decree absolute. Once you have received the certificate, you are officially divorced and free to marry again, if you so wish…

An important note at this point is that if you want a legally binding arrangement for dividing money and property (which you do), you must submit this request to the court before you apply for a decree absolute.

Getting a Divorce in Scotland

Two types of procedures can be used in Scotland to apply for divorce. These are often known as the *simplified* procedure and the *ordinary* procedure. If you meet the requirements of the simplified procedure, it will take around two months for the divorce to be complete. If you do not qualify, you will need to seek advice from a solicitor and follow the ordinary procedure.

To qualify for the simplified procedure, you need to have lived in Scotland for at least six months immediately before the application and be domiciled in Scotland. Additionally, you and your spouse need to have lived apart for at least one year and your spouse must consent to the divorce. If your spouse does not consent, you will qualify for this process if you have lived apart for two years. Lastly, there must be no children of the marriage under the age of 16, and neither you nor your spouse can claim any lump sum or maintenance payment.

Getting a Divorce in Northern Ireland

Applying for divorce is the same in Northern Ireland as it is in England and Wales. A divorce petition must be grounded on one of the same five reasons:

- Two years' separation with the consent of the other spouse to divorce.
- Five years' separation.
- Unreasonable behaviour.
- Adultery.
- Desertion.

If your wife agrees or is likely to conform to the divorce, you don't need to hire a solicitor. Instead, you can contact the Matrimonial Office for guidance on bringing a petition for divorce as a *personal petitioner*. However, you should contact a solicitor if your wife does not consent to divorce or if she defends the case after the petition was issued.

Proposed Changes to UK Divorce Law

Unreasonable behaviour is the most common ground for divorce in the UK. This reason is cited most often, because UK divorce law does not have a no-fault system. One party must blame the other to obtain a divorce unless they are prepared to wait a minimum period of two years.

To prove that a marriage has broken down due to unreasonable behaviour, the petitioner must show that the respondent has behaved in such a way that they cannot be expected to live together.

On the 9th April 2019, it was announced that changes to the law will be put before Parliament. One of the proposals for reform is to replace the requirement to provide evidence of unreasonable behaviour with a statement of irretrievable breakdown of the marriage. They also propose to remove the ability to contest a divorce.

If these changes are approved, obtaining a divorce will be quicker and more straightforward. Additionally, in all cases, you could file for divorce yourself without the need of a solicitor and thus minimize your legal costs. At the time of writing, no date has been set for the changes. The legislation is expected to be introduced as soon as parliamentary time allows.

In the meantime, unreasonable behaviour is your only option if you both don't want to wait two years to file for divorce. It's important to stress that the evidence for unreasonable behaviour doesn't have to be serious. Not sharing the same bed or being more focused on work than on the relationship will usually suffice.

Contact Arrangements

It is an unfortunate fact that many women frustrate a father's access to his children during and after the separation process. The reasons are complicated and varied and, in some situations where there is a genuine risk to the child, justified. However, in most cases, limiting access to children is not warranted. While it is impossible to accurately calculate how many women do this, for balance, let's assume it is equal to the number of men who turn their backs on their children following separation. If you are reading this book, I assume that you do not fall into this category, so let's explore the methods used to restrict access and discuss what you can do about it.

The inevitable disputes during separation can result in a breakdown of the relationship between the two parents, which can lead to problems of access. These problems can range from the child suddenly not being available when the father arrives to the mother moving away to prevent access altogether.

Children can feel conflicted spending time with you, because they think that they are hurting their mum. Sometimes mothers build on this and use it against the father, refusing access on the grounds that it creates too much trauma for the child.

Whatever the scenario, the bottom line is that you need to find a way to overcome these challenges, because in most cases, access is controlled by the resident parent. As 90% of resident parents are women, it is generally the father who finds himself in a position where he must negotiate access.

Collection and drop off can be some of the more challenging times, because you are likely to encounter your ex-partner then. Tempers may flare, resulting in a stressful experience for both parents and the children. You need to be more mindful and rehearse how a future meeting may play out. By assessing the potential scenarios of the contact, you can pre-empt possible hostilities and prepare an appropriate response.

If you have a volatile relationship and you lose your temper, you could be the subject of a police investigation. In a situation like this, your ex-partner could speak to her solicitor and try to reduce or cease contact altogether based on your behaviour. As you can imagine, it is critical that you keep calm, even if you are provoked.

So, what can do you do if you arrive to pick up your child and find that no one is home or that your ex-partner refuses access? I wish I could give you a satisfactory solution, but the truth is that there is absolutely nothing you can do about it in that immediate moment.

Even if you have a court order in place, in which the details of access are legally binding, the police would not force your partner to release the children to you. There is absolutely no recourse in UK law if the resident parent refuses to hand over the children.

The police will likely only attend to a situation like this in response to a Public Order Offence. Acting in a way that is found to be abusive, threatening or insulting carries a maximum sentence of six months' imprisonment. Abusive behaviour includes words, actions and even gestures or signs.

It is incredibly easy to get angry in a situation where you are prevented from seeing your children, but you must keep control of your emotions. While imprisonment is unlikely unless you do something stupid, you might easily give your ex-partner a reason to prevent you from having access to your children.

If you are prevented access, write a letter or email to your ex-partner to make a record of the breach. Keep a diary of every instance this occurs. If your children are old enough, communicate with them directly. Explain that you were there. Don't assign blame. Keep it simple and tell them that, for whatever reason, their mum would not allow you to see them, but you are trying to resolve it.

If your ex-partner is consistently restricting access, you need to try and understand what is going on and why it is happening. While every situation is different, there are common reasons. The most obvious one is money.

Your ex-partner may feel that you are not paying enough for your children. The logic goes, if you are not paying enough, then why should you have the privilege to see them? If you consider this perspective, you can see how this argument could be justified. However, access to children and maintenance payments are legally independent of each other. In other words, there are no legal grounds to stop access if maintenance payments are not received. That said, it is quite common for the resident parent to restrict access to children when negotiating the financial settlement with the non-resident parent.

Situations can also arise where the receiving parent is getting the proper amount of money as calculated by the CMS but pushes for more money. This, too, is a challenging scenario, and many fathers comply to maintain the relationship. If this happens to you, keep a record of it and don't give away what you can't afford.

Another primary reason that access is restricted is that your ex-partner no longer wants you in her life and may have found someone else. Think about it for a minute: she finds a new partner and wants to create a new life for herself and the children. Imagine the major inconvenience of having this picture-perfect scene repeatedly shattered by your ugly ass turning up and reminding her about a failed relationship.

I say this tongue-in-cheek, because although it is understandable for her to want to focus on her new life, you remain the father of your children. This situation can get worse if she tries to push her new partner as a replacement father for your children.

In either situation, there is nothing you can do immediately to resolve the problem. In fact, in any conflict concerning access, the only action you can ever immediately do is something that might jeopardise future access.

I know it is easy to feel sad, angry or hurt. You might feel like smashing stuff up. You might simply feel numb. But none of this will help you get what you want. Being a victim, being weak and letting someone else control you and your emotions will never get you what you want.

You must be strong and begin with the end in mind. When you know what you want, you instinctively make the right choices. Regular contact with your children: that is your number-one goal. If you make a bad move, you could be prevented and restricted legally from seeing your children. Do not let the actions of another person, irrespective of how wrong they might be, legally prevent you from seeing your children in the long term.

If you find yourself in this situation, breathe. Walk away if you must. Know that this and any other conflict is temporary. You could try to reason with her, but if she is pushing you out in this way, she will be unlikely to admit culpability for her actions. Instead, tell her that you are happy that she has moved on and that you want to make your contact as frictionless as possible. Keep turning up at previously agreed times, and keep a record of any deviations. Make sure your children know that you are trying to see them and that you are working hard to resolve the situation, but don't appoint blame.

Another potential reason for reducing access can be jealousy, which can be triggered for a host of reasons. A common one is that she thinks that you are enjoying yourself with no responsibilities whatsoever while she is struggling to bring up your children at home. In this situation, it is mutually beneficial that she gives you access, because you will get to spend time with your children while she gets more time for herself.

An additional common reason for access restriction is more challenging to resolve: plain, old revenge. Depending on your situation, your ex-partner might just want to make you suffer as much as possible. Restricting access to your children is an excellent way of doing so. Again, the best thing to do is keep calm, play the long game and let it blow over eventually. It will be challenging, but this is your best option given the circumstances.

If you find that you are not able to secure regular access, you might be considering pursuing the legal route. Before you do, however, make sure that you give the situation enough time to settle down. It is more common to suffer with problems of access in the early stages when emotions are still raw and the financial settlement is being negotiated. Document any issues and regularly review your records to see if the occurrences are reducing, increasing or staying the same. Analyse whether the incidents follow a pattern, as this might hold the key to finding a solution.

If the situation still does not improve after waiting it out, then you may have to choose the legal route. The courts now insist that you try mediation first, which can be a better and lower-cost option. If this doesn't work, your final choice is a court order, and you will need the support of a solicitor.

Not only does the court process take a long time, but it can also cost a lot of money. Even worse is that your ex-partner can breach the order with essentially no repercussions. The most severe consequence that she is likely to receive is a reprimand by the courts. The only remedy the court would employ in these circumstances is to send her to prison. I have not been able to find a single example where a mother was imprisoned for breach of a contact order, probably because of the impact on the children. For this reason, you should avoid a court order for access if possible. The best possible outcome for everyone concerned is for the parents to informally agree between themselves on access to the children.

Summary

Divorce can be extremely costly, but with the right preparation, you can minimise the expense. The divorce process is very straightforward and does not require the help of solicitors if your wife agrees to the divorce.

Wherever possible, agree on the financial arrangements informally with your wife, and then use a solicitor to draft the settlement plan for the court to approve. Take your time with this and be fair but sensible. You do not have to give everything away.

For assets and liabilities that have yet to be split, put temporary arrangements in place if necessary. Ensure that you make it clear that the arrangement is temporary until the final agreement.

The financial consent order must provide a clean break to prevent either party from trying to add or take away something at a later date. To be legally binding, this request must be submitted to the court before you apply for the decree absolute.

Securing access to children is the most ineffective element of the legal process and must be avoided at all costs. If your ex-partner is currently restricting access, refrain from doing anything that could legally jeopardise access to your children.

I know it seems counterintuitive, but you must overcome any problems that you had with your child's mother and establish a new style of relationship where you work together as partners to bring up your children.

You are facing some of the biggest challenges a man can face. Just know that whatever the current status, the situation will be resolved. Stay positive and persistent, and you will reach a favourable outcome.

CHAPTER 6:
MANAGING YOUR FINANCES

Child Maintenance

The purpose of child maintenance is to provide support for a child's everyday living costs. The non-resident parent must make payments to the resident parent, who is responsible for the child's day-to-day care.

There are three ways to determine how much maintenance you will pay for your children:

1. Decide informally with your ex-partner.
2. Hire solicitors to help you reach an agreement.
3. Have the Child Maintenance Service (CMS) calculate the amount.

Working out the amount with your ex-partner is a practical method; consider using a mediation service if you are having difficulty communicating. However, this informal approach carries a level of uncertainty, as either party can revisit the amount at any time in the future.

Agreeing on an arrangement using the help of solicitors will be costly but may be necessary if your finances are complex. You can also ask the court to make the child maintenance payments legally binding. This approach might be useful if you anticipate becoming increasingly wealthy. The downside is that if your circumstances take a turn for the worst, you would still be legally required to pay the agreed amount.

The CMS has come under fire in some circles, but in my experience, they are quite straightforward, and their calculations are transparent and fair.

Along with limited access to children, maintenance payments create the most frustration amongst fathers. Some argue that they are happy to pay for their children, but they want all of the money spent directly on their children.

In these circumstances, it is helpful to consider that your separation should not result in suffering for your children and their mother. When you were all together, you enjoyed a certain kind of lifestyle, which should continue where possible.

If you still earn the same amount of money as you did when your family was together, the CMS will calculate an amount that should maintain the lifestyle enjoyed by your children. This includes the type of home your children live in and the type of activities that they can enjoy.

How the CMS Calculates Child Maintenance

The Child Maintenance Service follows six steps to calculate the amount of child maintenance you will pay. The amount is reviewed every year and can change based on changes in income or family circumstances.

Step 1. Working out Your Annual Gross Income

The CMS works out child maintenance using your taxable annual gross income as the starting point. Income includes earnings from employment, self-employment (profits from a business), occupational or personal pensions and certain benefits. Annual gross income is your yearly income before income tax and National Insurance have been withdrawn, but after your employer or personal pension scheme deductions.

The figures are usually taken from HM Revenue & Customs (HMRC). HMRC uses the information from your last complete tax year, which runs from 6th April in one year to 5th April in the next.

It is possible that your circumstances have changed in your current tax year. Perhaps, for example, you received a bonus in the taxable year that you do not expect to receive this year. Unfortunately, the CMS will still calculate your annual gross income at this higher level, unless the previous income level is 25% higher than that from the current year.

Step 2. Items that Reduce Your Weekly Gross Income

Your gross income in Step 1 can be adjusted if:

- You make payments into a personal pension scheme.
- You have certain costs or expenses.

Contributions into an employer pension scheme are accounted for in Step 1, but if you pay into a private pension, you should deduct it here. For example, if you have a gross income of £27,000 a year and make annual private pension contributions of £1000, the amount of gross income the CMS will consider is £26,000.

Gross Income	£27,000.00
Less	
Personal Pension Payment	£1,000.00
Considered Gross Income	£26,000.00

You can ask the CMS to consider certain costs or expenses that can reduce the gross income figure used to calculate child maintenance. You can apply for a *special expenses variation* for the following:

- Travel costs to maintain regular contact with your child (if more than £10 a week)
- Costs connected with supporting a child with a disability or a long-term illness
- Repaying debts from your former relationship, for example, a car loan for a car the receiving parent has kept
- Boarding school fees for children who qualify for child maintenance
- Paying the mortgage for the property where the receiving parent and child live

After taking personal pension contributions and variations into account, the CMS converts considered gross income into a weekly gross income. This is done by dividing gross income by 365 days and multiplying that number by 7.

Considered Gross Income	£26,000.00
Divided by 365 Days	£71.23
Multiplied by 7	£498.63

A gross income of £26,000 would be equal to a weekly gross income of £498.63.

This weekly figure allows the CMS to make additional reductions based on any other children you support. If you have other children, the CMS will reduce your weekly gross income by the following percentage:

- 11% reduction for one child
- 14% reduction for two children
- 16% reduction for three or more children

For example, if you support one other child, your weekly gross income would be reduced by 11%, leaving a considered weekly income of £443.78.

Weekly Gross Income	£498.63
Less	
11% Reduction for 1 Child	£54.85
Considered Weekly Income	£443.78

Step 3. Determining the Child Maintenance Rates

Child maintenance rates are assigned based on your gross weekly income:

Maintenance Rate	Weekly Income Band
Basic	£200.00 to £800.00
Basic Plus	£800.01 to £3,000.00 (Basic rate applied to first £800)
Reduced	£100.01 to £199.99
Flat	£7 to £100 (Or receives benefits)
Nil	Less than £7

In our example, £443.78 would fall under the Basic child maintenance rate.

Step 4. Assigning the Number of Children to Receive Child Maintenance

The CMS applies the number of children who have been included in the application for child maintenance.

Step 5. Calculating the Weekly Amount of Child Maintenance

Basic Rate

The Basic rate applies if your gross weekly income after Step 2 is £200 to £800. The amount of child maintenance you will pay each week is based on the following percentages:

- 12% for one child
- 16% for two children
- 19% for three or more children

For example, if you have two children and a gross weekly income of £443.78 at Step 2, you would pay 16% of your gross weekly income, or £71 per week.

Considered Weekly Income	£443.78
Basic Rate at 16% Payable for 2 Children	
Child Maintenance Due per Week	£71.00

Basic Plus Rate

If your gross weekly income after Step 2 is more than £800 up to a limit of £3,000, the Basic Plus rate of child maintenance is applied as well as the Basic rate. In addition to the percentage rates applied to the first £800 above, the following percentages are calculated on any balance over £800:

- 9% for one child
- 12% for two children
- 15% for three or more children

For example, if you had two children and a gross weekly income of £1000, you would pay £152.00 per week.

Considered Weekly Income	£1,000.00
Basic Rate up to £800	
16% of £800 for 2 Children	£128.00
Basic Plus Rate £800.01 - £1000	
12% of £199.99 for 2 Children	£24.00
Child Maintenance Due per Week	£152.00

Reduced Rate

If your gross weekly income after Step 2 is more than £100 but less than £200, you would pay a fixed rate of £7 a week for the first £100 and the following percentage will be applied to the balance:

- 17% for one child
- 25% for two children

- 31% for three or more children

For example, if you had two children and a gross weekly income of £150 at Step 2, you would pay £19.50.

Considered Weekly Income	£150.00
Flat Rate up to £100 at £7	£7.00
Reduced Rate £100.01 - £150	
25% of £49.99 for 2 Children	£12.50
Child Maintenance Due per Week	£19.50

Flat Rate and Nil Rate

If your weekly gross income is less than £100 or you or your partner receive certain benefits, you would pay a flat rate of £7 a week in child maintenance.

If you are under 16, a student aged 19 or less, in prison or in a care home, you would not have to pay any child maintenance.

Step 6. Shared Care

If your child stays overnight with you at least one night per week on average, you will receive a reduction in the amount of child maintenance you pay. The more nights that your children stay overnight with you, the more the CMS will reduce the weekly amount of child maintenance:

Number of Nights	Reduction
52 to 103	1/7
104 to 155	2/7
156 to 174	3/7
More than 175	(50%) plus an extra £7 a week for each child

For example, if your children stay with you on Friday and Saturday night each fortnight, this would add up to 52 nights per year. The amount of weekly child maintenance due would be reduced by one-seventh.

Child Maintenance Due per Week	£152.00
Less	
1/7 Reduction for 52 Nights of Care	£21.71
Child Maintenance due per week	£130.28

Payment of the Child Maintenance

Once your child maintenance payments have been calculated, you will receive a letter that provides a breakdown of the information used to reach this amount. You can choose to use the *Direct Pay* method to deposit the correct amount into your ex-partner's account each month.

The alternative is the *Collect and Pay* service, which you should avoid at all costs. Here, the CMS collects the amount from your bank account or directly from your employer. Not only is this potentially embarrassing, but the fees are also punitive.

The paying parent is charged a 20% fee on the child maintenance payment, and the receiving parent has 4% subtracted from the payment.

You will pay child maintenance until your child is at least 16 years old, unless they decide to continue with full-time education. This includes A levels but does not include university or professional studies. The payments will end when the course finishes or when the child turns 20 years old, whichever is sooner.

Parentage

The Child Maintenance Service (CMS) assumes that you are the parent if:

- You were married to the child's mother at any time between the conception and birth of the child (unless the child was adopted)
- You are named on the child's birth certificate (unless the child was adopted)
- You have taken a DNA test that shows you are the parent
- You have legally adopted the child
- You were named in a court order as the parent when the child was born to a surrogate mother

If parentage is assumed, the CMS will work out the amount of child maintenance to be paid. You will have to pay this amount unless you can prove that you are not the parent.

If you deny that you are the parent of a child, the CMS will ask for evidence, and they may ask you to take a DNA test. You will have to continue paying the calculated child maintenance amount until you can prove that you are not the father. The CMS may refund any payments made after the date that you first denied being the parent if you can confirm your claim.

If the amount of child maintenance has yet to be calculated, then you will not have to make any payments until the disagreement has been resolved. However, if you are found to be the parent, the amount of child maintenance you must pay will be backdated.

Penalties for Non-Payment of Child Maintenance

Penalties for not paying child maintenance are severe. The Child Maintenance Service can take the one-off or regular payments directly from your salary, bank or building society without your permission. The CMS can also take court action, which can result in bailiffs being instructed to remove and sell your belongings. You can be put in prison for up to six weeks and forced to sell your house to pay for the child maintenance owed.

Budget Planning

You will likely find yourself with less money than you had previously. If you haven't done so already, it is time to take control of your finances by creating a budget plan. You can get a free copy of the budget plan on my website at www.realmansdivorce.com, or you can create your own in a spreadsheet or even on paper.

The first step is to calculate your income. Use net income, which is income after taxes and other deductions. If you have regular income from another source, such as rental income from a property, add this too.

Now you need to calculate your necessities. These are the outgoings that you must pay each month. First, include your rent or mortgage costs and other occupancy costs, such as council tax, water, gas and electricity. If you have additional properties, don't forget to add your landlord costs, such as your mortgage and management fees.

Next, add miscellaneous expenses, such as your mobile phone, broadband, TV license and subscriptions including iTunes, Spotify, Netflix, and cable TV. Include insurance policies, such as car, home, travel and life insurance.

The average UK household debt is currently at £15,400, so you likely have some debt to manage. If you have debt, include a repayment section showing monthly payments towards credit cards and unsecured loans. Over this challenging period, you will need to find a way to reduce existing debt and avoid racking up any further liabilities.

Calculate travel costs as well, whether for car lease repayments and fuel or train fares. Don't forget to include the costs to see your children, and include hotel costs if your children live away from your home. Work out your weekly spending on food and clothes. Again, don't forget to factor in the cost of food if you travel to see your children and any clothing costs for them. If you have a personal pension or regular savings, add them in.

If you know your monthly child maintenance costs, add this in or estimate it using the information in the last section.

Add any additional costs. Maybe haircuts and a gym membership are essential for you. Your list should be specific for you, so include anything that you feel is a necessity.

Once you have included all your necessities, subtract them from your income. The target is that your outgoings don't exceed more than 70% of your income. This likely won't be the case, so you may want to reduce some of your costs.

If you live on your own, you can apply for a single person's discount on your council tax. Consider switching the supplier of your gas and electricity to get a better deal. If you use a specialist website, they will take care of all of the logistics.

Can you get a better deal on your mobile phone? Do you need all of those TV channels? Can you save money by buying your groceries elsewhere? Now is the time to review your expenses to determine whether you are getting the best deals.

Money Management Strategy

Most people have one bank account to receive their salary, pay their bills and fund any additional spending. With outgoings leaving your account on different dates throughout the month, it's difficult to understand your exact financial position and it's easy to overspend.

We tend to only think about saving money once we have finished spending each month. This approach is the exact opposite of how we should manage our money. Our savings, the money that will sustain us and one day make us financially free, are the first thing we should take out of our income.

To do this, you need to set up some additional bank accounts, which is fairly straightforward if you have online banking. If you haven't or if your bank doesn't support this, switch to a bank that does.

Create a *freedom* account for your savings and investments and decided on an amount that you will save each month. A rule of thumb is 10% of your income, so if you earn £1500 a month, you would save £150.

You don't have to be a market expert to invest your money. Rather than selecting individual stocks yourself or paying an expensive fund manager to try to beat the market, you can invest in a low-cost index tracker fund. These funds track an index, or a group of stocks, commonly major stock markets such as the FTSE100 in the UK or the S&P500 in the US.

These indexes contain well-known household companies, such as BP, Sainsbury's and Unilever. By investing in these trackers, you are betting that you and your fellow countrymen will continue to use these companies' products and services. These are the businesses that drive our economy.

Of course, the stock market can go down as well as up, but index trackers are a long-term investment, and history has shown that major markets such as the FTSE have always recovered any downturn.

Create a *future* account to save money for things that you know you will buy in the future, such as a holiday or a deposit for a mortgage or to pay for car maintenance. I'm not a financial advisor, but I don't need to be one to understand that paying interest on a credit card for a holiday will cost me more than if I pay for it with my own money. This is the purpose of a future account. The idea is to free you from having to borrow money from the banks, who will charge you a fortune in interest.

That isn't to say that credit cards can't be useful. There's good debt and bad debt. Good debt is where you use that money to generate more wealth. For example, you can get 0% interest money transfers and balanced transfer deals for up to three years that you can use on existing debt. Rather than paying 18% interest on existing debt, you can transfer it to one of those cards, thus reducing the amount of money that you have to pay back.

Bad debt is where you live off of a credit card. If you don't pay the full balance each month, you are effectively increasing the cost of what you bought by 18% or more. That is worth considering when you see something on sale!

The next account should bring you enjoyment: your *fun* account. This is money that you will use every month to have fun. Whether it's a weekend at a theme park with the children or a deep-tissue massage for yourself, use this money to do something that will make you feel good, guilt-free. You have taken care of your necessities, your future and your medium-term needs, so this account is your reward. Again, the target here is 10%.

This strategy will help you take control of your finances and safeguard your future. You might have some work to do to reduce your spending on necessities to less than 70% of your income, as stated in the section above. If reaching this target is impossible, reduce the percentage contribution to the freedom, future and fun accounts. The most important account is the freedom account, as only this one can make you financially free. Even if you start with only 1% of your income, save it to develop the habit. As your finances improve, increase your contribution to your various accounts. Don't make the mistake of waiting to have money before you manage it. Manage your money now, and then you will have it. It's not about the amount; it's about the habit.

The Money Management Strategy increases awareness of your current financial situation so that you can make informed choices on how you spend your money, how you save your money and how you will use your money in the future.

As a father, I love the benefit that this process will have on my children. No classroom teaches children about money, so we must show them. Children learn best from modeling what we do, so what better way to teach them than to demonstrate the strategies above?

Calculating Net Worth

You will find calculating your net worth very useful. Net worth tells you precisely what your current financial position is. You will likely be asked for this information when you try to agree on a financial settlement with your ex-partner.

The net worth calculation evaluates your assets and your liabilities. Assets are anything of value that you own, and liabilities are anything that you owe to somebody else. The calculation for net worth is your total assets minus your total liabilities.

If the net worth figure is positive, it means that you own more than you owe. If the number is negative, you owe more than you own. For example, if you have £250,000 in assets and £200,000 in liabilities, you would have a positive net worth of £50,000.

Assets	£250,000
Less	
Liabilities	£200,000
Net Worth	£50,000

If you have £200,000 in assets and £250,000 in liabilities, you would have a negative net worth of £50,000.

Assets	£200,000
Less	
Liabilities	£250,000
Net Worth	-£50,000

A negative net worth does not necessarily mean that you are financially irresponsible. However, it does mean that, currently, you have more liabilities than assets. Your net worth will fluctuate over time; however, it is vital that the overall trend increases over time.

Ideally, as we age, our net worth will continue to grow as we gain equity in our home, pay back debt and acquire more assets. However, at certain points, it is normal for our net worth to fall, for example, when we get divorced or when we start to tap into savings and investments for our retirement.

So, what should your net worth be? It is impossible to create a formula that works for everyone, because each person's financial situation is different. That said, if most people in the UK have finished their studies and are in full-time employment by age 25, a reasonable calculation would be:

Target Net Worth = (Age − 25) x (Gross Annual Income / 5)

For example, if you were 40 years old with an average gross income of £40,000, your target net worth would be £120,000.

$$£120,000 = (40 - 25) \times (£40,000 / 5)$$

Remember, this formula is to be used simply as a starting point. Your ideal net worth may be more or less depending on your lifestyle and goals. Once you understand your current position, you can act accordingly. Average interest rates in a savings account with a UK bank are around 1%. If you have money in a savings account that is earning low levels of interest, it might better to use it to clear a loan or credit card debt that is charging you a much higher rate of interest.

Monitoring your net worth over time can motivate you to continue with your strategy. On the other hand, if the results are not in line with your expectations, it can encourage you to take further action.

For convenience, I have provided a free Net Worth Tracking template on my website www.realmansdivorce.com. You may find it helpful to download a copy before I walk you through it in the next segment.

There are four types of assets:

1. Cash and Liquid Assets. This is money in your bank accounts and any cash that you have on hand.
2. Marketable Assets. These are investments, such as stocks and property, that you intend to sell at some point to generate cash.
3. Long-Term Assets. These are investments that you do not intend to convert to cash in the short term, such as pensions or life insurance.
4. Personal Assets. These are the assets that you own and enjoy the use of, such as the property that you live in, your car, household furnishings and so on.

The total value of all of these components is your total asset value.

There are two types of liabilities:

1. Short-term debt such as credit cards, overdrafts, unpaid bills and loans.
2. Long-term debt such as the mortgage on your home.
   The total value of these components is your total liabilities.

By subtracting your liabilities from your assets, you can determine your net worth. The courts may want to see these figures when establishing any settlement between you and your ex-partner.

Summary

When you make child maintenance payments, you are ensuring that your child's standard of living is maintained. This means that their health, education and general wellbeing are also sustained. Most men, certainly those who are reading this book, recognise and accept that they should pay towards their child's upbringing. However, some do think that the amount is too much and feel that they are not left with enough money.

Try to view your child support payments as benefiting your child, not your ex-partner. The aim is for your child to maintain the same standard of living as when you were together. Why should your child suffer because of the split? Even if your ex-partner is withholding contact, do not withhold payment. If you do, you will be hurting your child twice. Take the moral high ground and know that you can look your child in the eye with a clear conscience.

CHAPTER 7:
IMPROVING YOUR HEALTH AND FITNESS

I'm not a dietician or fitness professional, but I do know a thing or two about getting in shape. In January 2017, I found myself three months away from the start line of the Marathon Des Sables, and I was barely managing to run 15 miles a week.

The Marathon Des Sables is known as the world's toughest foot race. It is a 250km, 6-day race across the Sahara Desert. It's a marathon each day except on the "long" day, which exceeds two marathons. All while carrying your week's food and equipment on your back in temperatures of up to 50 degrees Celsius.

I should have started training at least a year earlier, building a base level of fitness that equalled about 30-40 miles of running a week before commencing a 24-week schedule that took my weekly mileage to over 70 miles a week.

Instead, I found myself overweight and out of shape in a cold, British winter. I won't go into the specific training, but I eventually reached the start line in pretty good shape and, more importantly, injury free. Some of the best runners on the planet run this race, and I managed to finish in 180th place overall and in 66th place for my age group.

I do have a history of fitness, and I have trained for many events over the years, but I also have a history of being out of shape. This has provided me with a lot of experience in getting back into peak condition. In fact, as I write this, I need to lose two stones and rebuild my fitness after 6 months of forced rest to recover from a back injury. So once again, I'm implementing the advice that follows.

If we want to achieve and sustain a healthy weight, we need to understand some fundamentals. I'll keep this section as accessible and punchy as possible, but if you want to understand the science in more detail, you can find more resources at www.realmansdivorce.com.

Most of us could stand to lose a few pounds; some more than others. In modern life, particularly when you're in a serious relationship, it is so easy to opt for speed and comfort rather than what is good for you. Ready meals, takeaways and the growing popularity of delivery services mean that you can get pretty much any meal delivered to your door. Fitting exercise in or, rather, finding the motivation to exercise within our busy lifestyles is challenging. Now that you have separated from your ex-partner, you might find that you are in pretty bad shape.

Maybe you are not much of a cook, or maybe your partner did all of the cooking. Perhaps you both lived on ready meals or takeaways. Whatever your previous situation was, now you need to look after yourself. The food, the type of fuel that you consume is vital. Our bodies and minds are connected to each other. How your body feels will have a knock-on effect on your mind. If you want to feel better as well as look better, you have to take care of your body.

We will tackle this topic in a couple of ways. We will start with some fundamental laws of fat burning to help you understand how you can reduce excess body fat and get into shape. We will then explore the main components of a healthy lifestyle, starting with diet and the types of food that you should and shouldn't be eating, before covering exercise. Finally, I will give you a quick fix to drastically shift body fat and improve your appearance, your mood and your outlook on the world.

The Laws of Fat Burning

The recommended average calorie intake for men is 2500 per day, which is determined by individual size and activity levels. Carbohydrates are our bodies' primary source of energy. We find them in foods such as pasta, bread and potatoes. One gram of carbs contains four calories. Protein, whether found in meat or vegetables, also has four calories per gram. Fats are more nutritionally dense and have nine calories per gram. Alcohol, for those curious, contains seven calories per gram.

Contrary to what some advertisements would have you believe, there is no secret formula for fat loss. To lose body fat, we must eat fewer calories than our body needs. When we do this, our bodies switch from carbohydrates as their preferred source of energy to the fat that we have stored around our bodies. It is that simple. There is no other way of burning fat.

If you consume the same amount of calories as your body needs, your weight will stay the same. Consume more and your weight will go up; eat less and your weight will go down. People who have physically demanding jobs require more calories than those who are mainly deskbound. Adding exercise drives up your calorie requirement. Therefore, increasing the amount that you exercise while restricting calories reduces your body fat, as your body will use that fat to generate energy.

Exercise also increases muscle mass. Muscle burns more calories than fat, so the more muscle tissue we have, the more calories our bodies need each day to maintain that muscle. Using exercise to manage our weight is also beneficial, but the most effective way is via our diet. Thus, we will concentrate on that.

The easiest way to reduce calories is to eliminate excess fat from our diet. Remember that fat has nine calories per gram, so 100g of fat contains more than double the amount of calories than the same weight of carbohydrates or proteins. By reducing our fat consumption, we can eat more food that gives us a feeling of satiety.

Reduce fat by removing the skin from chicken, cutting visible fat off of red meats or choosing leaner cuts, like fillet steak. Substitute egg whites for whole eggs. If you eat scrambled eggs, use one whole egg and two egg whites. Avoid full-fat milk, yogurts and cheese. Reduce or eliminate butter, oils and salad dressings, or opt for a lower fat version. I know that you know this already, but biscuits, cakes and pies do not have a regular place in a healthy diet.

Not all fats are harmful; some are an essential part of a healthy diet. Eat oily fish, like salmon and sardines, as well as nuts and avocados, but keep them to a minimum when you are trying to lose body fat.

An effective way of burning body fat is to control a hormone in our body called insulin. Insulin is released by the body when we consume carbohydrates. How significantly insulin rises depends on the type of carbohydrates we eat. Refined carbs, such as biscuits and sugary foods, are digested quickly and raise insulin levels substantially.

We need to avoid these foods, because after our insulin levels spike, they drop. This decline sends a signal to our brain that we need more food, and we experience hunger pangs.

The classic, full English breakfast has a deserving title of "heart attack on a plate," but don't be fooled into thinking that breakfast cereal is a healthy alternative. Many kinds of cereal contain far too much sugar. The sugar fires up our insulin levels, and then a few hours later, we feel hungry again and start reaching for the chocolate or crisps.

A clever trick is to never eat carbs by themselves. This rule will stop you from eating sweets, and it has a broader application as well. Take breakfast cereal as an example. Using this rule, you would need to add fat or protein. Doing so might be challenging, so a better option would be scrambled eggs with a small slice of wholemeal bread and some low-fat spread. This will keep you satisfied for much longer because you are controlling your insulin level.

There is another reason why we should manage our insulin levels. To maintain pace, I won't go into the science of it, but just know that high levels of insulin actually convert the carbohydrates we eat into fat. Therefore, if we eat the wrong types of carbs, our insulin levels increase, which can potentially lead to more fat being stored on our body. To make matters worse, high levels of insulin switch off our body's ability to burn body fat.

Avoid carbs such as white bread, cereals, sweets, white rice, white potatoes and pasta. If you only employ one change to your diet, your greatest success will come from eliminating or drastically reducing these kinds of carbohydrates. Instead, eat such carbs as porridge, sweet potatoes and pulses, which are digested slowly and, thus, don't raise insulin levels as much.

Dietary Guidelines for a Long and Healthy Life

We all know the saying, "You are what you eat," and we know that we must avoid junk food. However, many of us don't realise the full impact that food has on our bodies. We can see the effects food has on our physical appearance, but hidden from sight is the impact that food has at a cellular level. For instance, poor nutrition can impact our mood. People who eat fast food and pastries have a 51% increased chance of suffering from depression.

Nutrition is the most crucial factor that we can control that affects how long we live and the quality of our lives. Poor nutrition increases the likelihood that we will be diagnosed with certain major diseases and that we will grow old and frail in later life rather than staying active and energetic.

Indeed, more and more research is being released indicating that food can prevent and even reverse diseases such as diabetes, cardiovascular disease and Alzheimer's.

When the World Health Organisation released its findings that processed meats such as bacon and sausage are as dangerous to our health as cigarettes, it didn't take long for the jokes to circulate about how people would rather die young than eat a diet without such foods. What follows is a recommendation, a target to strive for based on solid research. If you want to treat yourself to a bacon sandwich or a slice of cake every now and then, go for it. Just try to eat healthy most of the time.

Eat a pescatarian diet, a plant- and fish-based diet, but only eat fish two to three times per week. Avoid large fish like tuna, because they contain high levels of mercury, which is hazardous to your health.

Most people overeat protein, which can lead to kidney damage. Reduce your daily intake to around 0.35g of protein per pound of body weight. If you weigh 150lbs, you should eat 53g of protein per day. Your diet should be free of animal proteins (red and white meat and cheese). Instead, your protein should come from vegetables such as legumes and nuts.

Reduce consumption of saturated, hydrogenated and trans fats. These products are found in processed foods, so start reading the labels. Instead, eat a diet rich in unsaturated fats, such as those found in olive oil and fish. These foods contain essential fatty acids called omega-3 and omega-6, which every cell in our bodies needs to function.

Eat complex carbohydrates, such as wholemeal bread and vegetables, and reduce your sugar intake by limiting refined carbohydrates, such as white bread, pasta, rice, cakes and fruit juices. Drinking fresh fruit juices, even the ones with bits in them, is not a healthy choice. Fruit juice contains as much sugar as most soft drinks. Always eat, rather than drink, fruit.

In addition to the three primary macronutrients, we need micronutrients such as vitamins and minerals. A diet rich in vegetables, fish, nuts and whole grains is the ideal way to get all of the essential nutrients. However, even with such a diet, it is possible to be deficient in vitamin D.

Vitamin D is essential for healthy bones. Our bodies cannot make vitamin D, so we need to get it from food or from exposure to sunlight. In the UK, most people can acquire sufficient vitamin D from sunlight exposure during the summer, but during autumn and winter, we are likely to have a deficiency that can cause bones to become soft and weak. During these months, consider taking a good multivitamin that contains vitamin D.

Flexitarian, vegetarian and vegan diets have become quite popular over the last few years, and food producers and restaurants now offer an incredible array of non-meat and non-dairy options. Just because something contains no meat, it does not mean it's necessarily healthier, especially if it's been processed. If a product is wrapped in an attractive package and requires heating up in a microwave or an oven, it is processed.

Irrespective of the promises on the packaging, processed food is never as healthy as the food you make yourself. Eating healthy has less to do with meat itself and more to do with production.

While it's true that the cheapest foods tend to be processed and unhealthy, it doesn't mean healthy eating can't be affordable. If you reduce your consumption of processed foods and meats and focus on fresh vegetables and fruit, your food bill will be lower. Shop around and buy direct from markets for the best prices.

The more you purchase (or grow) food in its most natural form to cook with, the healthier your diet will be. So learn to cook. If you can read or follow instructions on a video, you can cook. People have been doing it for millennia with less equipment than you have in your kitchen. Start on the weekends when you have more time. Challenge yourself to prepare one new dish a week until you get the hang of it.

I didn't eat red meat frequently, but I did eat chicken and eggs. I tried going vegan for a while and found it tough. Eventually, I got used to the vegan cheese, but I struggled with non-diary milk, and I missed eggs. Now I'm more relaxed. I try to eat a predominately plant-based diet, but if I want meat or dairy, I'll eat it too.

If you continue to eat meat, limit your consumption to once a day and combine the meat with water-rich food, such as a salad or steamed vegetables. Try to avoid red meats and steer clear of processed meats like bacon and sausages.

Drinking Water

The most critical element to our health is oxygen. Without it, we die in minutes. The second most important element is water. It is the largest, single component in our body. Our brain and heart are over 70% water, and our blood is more than 80% water. Digestion, circulation, excretion and other critical processes cannot occur without it.

Make sure you drink enough water to help your body function more efficiently. Aim for two litres spread across the day. If you exercise, you will need to drink more. Drinks containing caffeine, such as tea and coffee, and sugary drinks like sodas and fruit juices don't count, I'm afraid. Be aware that caffeine and alcohol affect the way that water is utilised in the body, thus increasing the need for more water.

A good indicator of whether you are drinking enough water is the colour of your urine. It should be clear. If there is any colour, drink some water. If you take a multivitamin or eat vitamin B2-rich foods, like asparagus, your urine can turn bright yellow. Don't worry; your body is just excreting the excess B2 from your body.

The best way to remember to drink water is to set your alarm on your phone. I ask Siri to remind me, which is even easier. As soon as I wake up, I drink a pint of water with a whole lemon squeezed into it to give me a vitamin C boost. Then, my phone reminds me to drink water throughout the day.

Exercise

We know we should exercise, but sometimes we think that we don't have enough time or money or perhaps we feel intimidated to start. The truth is that you can exercise anywhere, with little or no equipment, on your own or in groups.

The physical benefits of exercise are well documented, but it goes deeper than that. If you are feeling down or stressed out, or you simply want to give yourself a boost, exercise really is the best medicine. Doctors and healthcare professionals agree that exercise is one of the most effective ways to treat a wide range of mental health issues like depression and panic attacks. In many studies, exercise has been shown to be as effective as medication.

Everyone has ups and downs in their lives. I've been in situations where problems escalated until I felt that I had reached my breaking point. The circumstances in each case were different, but the common thread through all was a realisation that I needed to clear my head and make myself feel better through exercise.

For health, the best exercise is one that you enjoy and that you can fit into your busy lifestyle. The type of activity isn't important;

what is essential is that you use your whole body and raise your heart rate and breathing. The minimum amount of exercise should be 150 minutes of moderate intensity over two or more sessions per week. This can seem like a lot, but with some simple changes, it's easily accomplished.

One of the easiest and most accessible ways to get more exercise is to walk. Take the stairs, walk on the escalator, walk to work or take a walk at lunchtime. The day provides ample opportunities to walk. On the weekend, get outdoors and go for a long, brisk walk or, even better, a hike to get the heart pumping.

Running is one of the best forms of exercise that you can do. If you haven't run before or in a while, ease yourself into it. The beauty of running is that you can do it anywhere, whenever you want. That said, there are friendly running clubs all around the country that are always looking for new members. These clubs are a great way to meet new people and get fit.

Every weekend, almost 600 Parkruns take place around the country. Parkrun is a 5km walk, jog or run held on a Saturday morning. The events are run by volunteers and are completely free. You can join here at https://www.parkrun.org.uk/register/. Once registered, you will receive a barcode that you can scan at the end of each run to see your results.

While the ethos of Parkrun is to take part rather than to race, there is no better way to improve your speed and fitness than by running in a group. Some Parkruns attract hundreds of people, from children with their parents to centenarians. Whatever your level, you will gain the motivation to compete against others or your own time, or you can simply enjoy the camaraderie.

If you have children, exercise is an excellent way to have fun together. No doubt you've noticed that children have boundless energy and love to move. Raise your heart rate and smiles with classic children's games like tag and bulldog. Let your children take part in your activities, and if they show an interest in a sport, see if there is an opportunity to play with them.

Testosterone is a hormone produced in the body that is important for muscle and bone strength, sex drive and energy levels. Testosterone production starts to decrease from around age 30, but much of this decline is driven by lifestyle factors rather than age.

Stress, high insulin levels, alcohol consumption and chemicals such as BPAs all reduce testosterone production in the body. The good news is that exercise can boost testosterone levels and keep them high into old age.

On the other hand, excessive cardio, such as long-distance running, may decrease testosterone levels. So if you think you may have low levels, don't exceed more than 40 miles of running per week. Instead, focus on weight training and high-intensity interval training (HiiT).

To boost testosterone, you need to lift heavy weights for a low number of repetitions. Work the entire body and focus on compound movements, such as squats, deadlifts and bench presses.

Lifting is a skill, and injury can occur if the exercises are not performed correctly. If you are unfamiliar with weight training, join a good gym and seek out a personal trainer to get you started. Good gyms will offer a complimentary introduction.

Potentially more accessible is high-intensity interval training, which is short bursts of intense effort. HiiT can take the form of circuit classes, boot camps or even short-distance sprints. These activities are effective at burning body fat and getting you quickly in shape, but they put a considerable strain on the body. If you are overweight, have a family history of cardiovascular disease or have not trained before, seek the advice of your doctor before commencing any HiiT.

Most of our testosterone is produced while we sleep. Interrupted or insufficient sleep can reduce testosterone levels by 20% to 30%, so make sure that you are getting quality shut-eye every night.

10-Day Detox

If you truly want to kick-start your health and fitness and lose some excess fat, I have a really incredible 10-day programme for you. I won't lie to you – it sounds like it will be challenging, but I assure you that if you stick with it, you will be able to get through it and it will become effortless.

Before I go into more detail, I should make it clear that I am not a health professional or a dietician. If you have any concerns about the effect that this or any diet may have on your health, you should consult a doctor first. I should also point out that this programme is a quick fix. It should only be followed for 10 days, but it can be repeated every six months.

There is a saying that complexity is the killer of execution, and the beauty of this plan is in its simplicity. Even if your current culinary level is pouring boiling water over instant noodles, you can do this. All you have to do is eat only fruits and vegetables for 10 days. That's it. It's as straightforward as that. You can drink water and tea too.

The first step is to prepare for it. Go to the supermarket and buy your fruits and vegetables. As soon as you decide to do this, start straight away. I urge you to begin now that you have read this. Don't wait until tomorrow to start. Go out now and get your fruit and vegetables, we can continue when you get back...

Got everything? Well done, and welcome back! If you have just bought your supplies, I know that you will ace this detox. How do I know? Because you have taken action. Most people will read this and tell themselves that they will do it later. If you wait, you allow your brain time to talk you out of it, to make excuses for why you shouldn't do it. Remember, the brain's purpose is to keep you safe in your comfort zone. Fight back! If you haven't already, go to the store!

This plan will be fairly tough for the first couple of days. Day one is okay. Day two and three will get a bit trickier, but after that, it starts to become more manageable.

This detox works because it's so simple. You don't have to worry about preparing special meals or weighing or measuring quantities. Eat any amount of fruit or vegetables except for potatoes. Don't worry about the amount of sugar in the fruit; it doesn't matter for the 10 days. You will see dramatic weight loss and improvement in your health.

For breakfast, I tend to have fruit salad, such as mango, avocado and papaya. Add some fresh mint if you like or substitute some kiwi or fresh pineapple. For snacks, carrots and bananas are handy. I find roasted vegetables are a saviour when the hunger pangs kick in. Simply cut carrots, parsnips, and sweet potatoes into one-centimetre wide sticks and roast them for 45 minutes in the oven at 180 degrees Celsius. You can download some more recipe ideas at www.realmansdivorce.com.

You may experience a headache by the end of the first day and into the second day as the toxins are flushed out of your body. It is essential to drink at least eight 250ml glasses of water as the day goes on.

Before I did this detox for the first time, I was a huge coffee drinker. I absolutely loved coffee. I would drink around six to seven cups of coffee every day. My favourite gadget was my Nespresso machine, and I'd spend a fortune each month on the coffee pods.

I was aware of some of the risks of drinking too much coffee, but it was one of those things that I never really wanted to give up. To be honest, I could not even imagine starting a day without coffee. After completing the 10-day challenge, I gave away my coffee machine, and I didn't have another coffee for about six months. Now I occasionally treat myself to a cup, but I never experience the craving to drink one or three upon waking like I used to.

On the fourth day, the diet will become easy, and you will find the body fat falling off of you. Everyone is different, but from my own experience and the experience of others, and assuming that you are more than 20lbs overweight, you can expect to lose a minimum of 10lbs over the 10 days.

Once you have completed the 10 days, ease back into different foods gently; for instance, add in some healthy oils and grains. My advice would be to continue with a healthy diet rather than a high-fat, highly processed diet to maintain the results that you have achieved.

Summary

Eating a healthy diet and exercising are the most important elements that we can control that determine the length and quality of our lives. If you eat well and exercise, you are likely to maintain a healthy weight with normal blood pressure and cholesterol levels.

In the UK, one person dies every three minutes because of heart disease. Instances of stroke, diabetes and cancer are on the rise, and they are affecting increasingly younger people.

The good news is that these diseases can be avoided and, in some instances, reversed through a combination of exercise and eating healthily. Besides, these habits make us feel better. They improve our mood, reduce stress and energise us.

Having a fit and healthy body results in being able to enjoy all of the opportunities that life holds. Having fun with your children, friends and loved ones is even more enjoyable if you have the energy and agility to keep up.

Scientists are finding that age truly is only a number. Many men in their 40s, 50s and beyond are holding back the aging process through diet and exercise, redefining what it means to age. You could be one of them.

CHAPTER 8:
ENRICHING YOUR SOCIAL LIFE

When my daughter was a baby, I worked long hours and often travelled with work. If I were flying to Asia, I would leave on a Saturday evening to be ready for work on Monday morning. I would cram as much as possible into the week and fly back late Friday evening and land around 6am on Saturday morning.

I would be desperate to get home, wishing the taxi ride from Heathrow to Bromley would end. After a tough week on her own with our baby, my wife would take a well-deserved rest, and I would take over for the weekend. I felt so guilty about being away from home that I would make the most of every minute with my daughter, resulting in a full and hectic weekend. On Monday morning, I would leave for the office, exhausted and quietly looking forward to five days of rest at work. It was a rather challenging life, but it felt normal.

The guilt that I felt from being away from home also meant that I seldom made time for friends. My focus was on my immediate family and on working as a means of providing for them. The consequence was that I lost some of my identity. I wasn't a man anymore; I was a husband and a father. I did not take care of myself or make any time for myself; instead, I continued pushing myself harder and taking on increasing levels of stress to get ahead and provide.

Thinking back on the situation reminds me of a quote from the Dalai Lama:

"Man... sacrifices his health in order to make money. Then he sacrifices money to recuperate his health. And then he is so anxious about the future that he does not enjoy the present; the result being that he does not live in the present or the future; he lives as if he is never going to die, and then dies having never really lived."

In my case, I definitely came last in the relationship with myself. As a result, I did not make time for my friends, which is true for many men as well. Women, however, are quite good at keeping in constant contact with friends. When children are young, life for mothers centres on baby clubs, so friendships commonly develop through those groups. Often, men get pulled into these circles as well and create new relationships with other men who have also been drawn in by their wives or girlfriends.

Usually, these people are perfectly nice, but your relationship with them is based on your child going to baby clubs, rather than on a shared male interest. I used to feel resentful that I only had time to spend with these acquaintances rather than with my real friends.

Dropping your real friends in favour of family friends or friends of your partner can leave you in a somewhat vulnerable position after the divorce. You may now find yourself in a situation where you no longer have anyone to turn to, because all of your friendships were through your partner, and these friends are more likely to support her during the separation.

Regardless of the current status of your friendships, the benefit of being separated is that you have more opportunities to expand your social life. Before, you likely had no time whatsoever due to work, your intimate partner, fatherhood, and DIY projects. Now, you suddenly find that you have an abundance of time, especially on the weekends. This additional free time can take some getting used to, and you may find that you have too much time on your hands.

So, what can you do? Well, let's start with what you should not do. Beware of hitting the booze too hard. If you are reading this book, it is unlikely that you're a teenager, so the day after a night of partying can be especially painful for you. Emotionally, you might not be feeling your best during your separation, so it's wise not to magnify that feeling with a hangover from hell.

Identifying Your Passions

A valuable starting point to determine what to do with your time is to grab a pen and some paper and brainstorm. At the top of the page, write: "What I would do if I had unlimited time and money." Think about your list in these terms so that you don't limit yourself. Otherwise, the voice in your head will automatically dismiss ideas as ridiculous or unachievable, and you won't write them down.

The purpose of this exercise is to identify your passions, the things that give you joy, whether big or small. I realise that for some of you, finding any joy at the moment might be a stretch, but stay with me. You might find it easier to think about what used to provide you with happiness.

Just thinking and writing down things that used to give you pleasure will raise your mood. As you recall happy memories, your spirits will lift. Even more compelling is that your list will take on meaning and provide you with direction. It will give you something positive to focus on. It will get you out of your own head and provide you with some level of certainty in what is usually an uncertain time.

When I wrote my list for the first time, I decided that I wanted to go to Ibiza. I partied often when I was younger, but I'd hung up my dancing shoes once I was married with children. Now I could do whatever I wanted, so Ibiza went on my list.

I asked myself again, "What else do I want to do?" and looked across the room at the boxes of old vinyl that I'd been dragging around the country for the last 25 years. I made a note to buy some Technics 1210s and start DJ'ing. Now I was getting into my stride. I'd always admired Nile Rogers and imagined myself knocking out one of his killer grooves on the bass guitar, so learning the bass went on my list. Then I thought about the concerts I used to go to and added going to gigs to my list.

There were other activities, of course, but completing this exercise helped me realise how important music is to me. It prompted me to remember that music had been a noteworthy part of my life.

Four years later, I still haven't attempted the bass guitar, I didn't buy any turntables, and I haven't been to Ibiza. But I did start going to gigs again. I probably see a band once a month, which is a significant part of my social life. The point is that whatever comes to your mind, write it down. You will unearth some gems.

Don't worry that some people might find it ridiculous; it is your list, and you don't have to share it. And you will have plenty of time to edit the list later. This exercise will lead you to feel optimistic and confident about the future and provide you with plenty of ideas on how to spend your free time.

Gaining Clarity on Your Ambitions

The next exercise is designed to help you find clarity on your ambitions and purpose in life. This is important because our potential is determined by our ambitions. Focus on what you genuinely want to do rather than what you think you must do or what someone else says you should do.

To gain maximum benefit from this exercise, you need to be in the right state of mind. The fastest and easiest way to do this is by changing your body. Put on some loud music and for at least 10 minutes, dance around, run or do whatever it takes to get your blood pumping and the endorphins flowing. You want to put yourself in a peak state where you feel ready for anything.

Now, take some paper and start brainstorming the things that you would like to achieve in your life. To help generate ideas, write down your thoughts to the following questions:

- How would I like to feel each day?
- What are the talents and qualities that I admire in other people?
- What activities make me lose track of time?
- What kind of environment do I thrive in?
- What would make the most significant difference in my life if I changed or reached for something?
- If I could not fail, what would I do with my life?
- How can I make the world a better place for my children?
- If I only had one year to live, what would I do and how would I like to be remembered?

Once you've brainstormed your ideas, start to group them together and formulate a list of specific, major goals. In life, we have two main options. We either let life take us down a path of its own choosing, or we can use life's momentum to propel ourselves to where we want to go. This exercise helps you identify and recognise that you have the courage to choose your own direction in life.

You might be asking yourself: What does passion and ambition have to do with being more social? Having an awareness of your ambitions and passions creates a positive outlook. Have you ever noticed how a person positively lights up when they talk about something they are passionate about? This is our objective, to be the person that radiates positivity and fun, the person that people want to be around. This will become your natural persona as you start working on your passions and ambitions. Even reviewing your list before a social event will improve your mindset, making you more open and receptive.

I'm a big believer in being clear about what your goals are, because what you think about is what you get. When you think about something, you attract it to yourself because you consciously and subconsciously make decisions to achieve that goal. It might appear as if you're simply drawing what you want towards you, but you are actually taking action towards your goal.

As a teenager, I discovered that what I wanted from my life was to see the world. As a result of this deep, burning desire, I travelled all around the world. Wherever I went, I would always try to do or see something new. I'm a runner, and I felt blessed that I could put on a pair of trainers and go running. I like photography too, so I would run early as the city was waking up, taking photos along the way.

Once I got married and my daughter was born, being away from home was a double-edged sword. Travelling was how I earned my money and supported my family, but the pain of being away from my daughter was immense. I started to plan my trips as tightly as possible. I stopped allowing myself any extra time to see or do something new. I lost my appreciation for new experiences. And I wasted opportunities.

One day, after I became separated, I suddenly realised that I didn't have to rush home. I became aware of how lucky I was and of the many opportunities available to me. It began slowly, but I found that the more I felt grateful for, the more awareness I gained. You will find that as your appreciation grows, you will begin to see more beautiful things. It is almost like being a child again: everything around you is new and exciting. This is a fantastic state of mind to be in.

When we're young and start to experience freedom from our parents, everything seems incredible. Sadly, as we age, we become jaded and lose that appreciation. A benefit I found with my separation was that I began to appreciate things more. When you are appreciative, you feel like you are living, that you are taking an active part in life rather than letting life just happen to you.

A year into my separation, I went to Australia to meet with some business partners. They had very kindly arranged for my team and me to climb the Sydney Harbour Bridge at dusk on Friday evening. It was March, and the weather was perfect.

Once you are clipped into your harness, you make your way slowly up to the top of the bridge and back again, which takes a couple of hours. For safety reasons, you cannot bring a phone or a camera, which forces you to appreciate the view with your own eyes rather than through a viewfinder. And what a magnificent view.

As the sun set and the lights from the buildings and from the traffic lit up the city below, I could see the iconic opera house and the orange and red sky falling into the sea. I can't think of another city in the world that is in such a beautiful location as Sydney is. It is absolutely stunning.

I was sharing this wonderful experience with a colleague, and as we soaked up the scene, he turned to me looking forlorn. He told me that he wished his wife was with him and that he felt guilty doing this without her. I thought about what he said for a moment and realised that I had lived my life in that same state of mind for the last eight years.

I always felt guilty about travelling somewhere and having a good time. I completely understood how he was feeling, and at that moment, I had a realisation. This mentality is not how we should treat ourselves. If we have been given a gift, like the chance to experience breath-taking sights, we are doing ourselves a disservice if we don't make the most of it.

Being More Social

It is a truism that you will learn who your friends are in difficult times. I'm generalising here, but from my point of view, men don't typically talk about their feelings and emotions. For me in particular, I felt that I had failed. Failed because I hadn't been able to keep my marriage together. I was embarrassed about this "failure," so I wasn't about to shout it from the rooftops or post about it on Facebook.

I remember calling my best man, Mark, whom I hadn't seen in ages. We've been friends for a very long time, the type of friendship where you can pick up right where you left off even if you haven't seen each other in months.

I asked him what he was doing on the weekend, and he said that he was coming back from a holiday in Italy. This was my opportunity to back out, so I told him we could catch up another time. However, he sensed that something was wrong and pushed me to share. Reluctantly, I murmured something about separating, at which point he sprang into action and insisted on meeting me.

We went out that Saturday and got pretty drunk, as you can imagine. I'll never forget how he dropped everything for me. Your friends will do the same for you, but you have to reach out to people no matter how difficult it is. Don't isolate yourself. Loneliness is a serious health risk.

Loneliness impairs immune function and increases inflammation, which can lead to heart disease. Studies have found that those without adequate social interaction are twice as likely to die prematurely. That is the same mortality risk as smoking.

What do you do in a situation where you don't have many friends close by or anyone to go out with? If that is the case, then your new situation will be one of the most significant blessings that you will look back on.

You cannot go through life without any friendships. Most of us are social animals: we need to interact with other people for happiness and health. Relying on one person, such as your partner, for all of your social engagements is a risky strategy.

Perhaps you identified this tendency as a determining factor when you completed the exercise in Chapter 2 on your contribution to your breakup. Maybe you became overly reliant on your partner because you put other friendships on the back burner.

If you truly have no one to turn to, it is time to look for opportunities to meet new people. Engage with work colleagues and organise drinks after work. If you have a specific interest, find a club to get involved in. Push yourself even if you are introverted and don't feel very comfortable in groups. Be proactive even if you just don't feel like it. In fact, in my experience, "not feeling like it" is usually a sign that I need to give myself an extra push and override my brain's attempts to keep me in my comfort zone.

Sometimes, when we are presented with social opportunities, we worry that they won't be enjoyable. Quite often, this concern stems from our preconceptions about the people who will be there or who we think will be present. We believe that we won't have anything in common with those people or that they won't like us. To paraphrase Henry Ford, "Whether you think they will or think they won't, you are right."

If you feel that you won't enjoy a social gathering, you are more likely to be withdrawn. If you assume that someone doesn't like you, you are unlikely to be friendly towards them, and you may even act outwardly hostile as a defence mechanism.

Unsurprisingly, people aren't drawn to this kind of behaviour, and such expectations often become a self-fulfilling prophecy.

If you are prone to such thoughts, a useful technique is to visualise how you would like an engagement to unfold. Imagine enjoying yourself and being open and friendly with the other guests. Picture the other people with smiles on their faces as you converse.

Top performers use visualisation to reach the peak in their fields. Studies have shown that the brain does not differentiate between a real memory and an imagined one. Therefore, if we visualise something with enough lucidity that it incites our emotions, our mind stores the thought as a real memory.

Visualising your preferred outcome reduces your anxiety, because you trick your mind into believing that you have already successfully experienced the situation, albeit in your mind.

But how do you manage social situations if you are naturally reserved? It's worth remembering that it is not necessary to be the centre of attention to be a great conversationalist. Indeed, most people like talking about themselves and sharing their thoughts and opinions. Use this information to your advantage.

The key to social success is to make people feel comfortable and to ask questions that encourage them to talk about themselves. You can chat about anything as long as you aren't negative or unpleasant. No one likes excessive negativity, so being negative about other people or situations can reflect poorly on you. Keep this in mind when talking about your ex-partner. If necessary, it is better to say less than to be negative.

Although people like to talk about themselves, no one wants to feel interrogated. A conversation is a two-way process. You must also share details about yourself and your opinions to build trust and rapport. Further, it's critical to respond to questions with an answer that will allow the other person to ask further questions to keep the conversation going.

People like people who are like them. Whether it's hailing from the same city, fancying the same holiday destination or even sharing the same star sign, it's incredible how similarities can boost rapport. Seek to find similarities, and, however trivial, let the other person know if you have something in common.

My mum always used to say, "Clothes don't make the man." Being my mum, she is right, of course. That said, appearance is still important. We will cover this subject in more detail in the next chapter, but for now, make sure that your look matches others in a social setting if you want to fit in.

Whether you rock up in ripped jeans while everyone else is suited and booted, or you arrive in a suit while others are in dress casual, the disparity will be noticeable. Although the gap is not usually insurmountable, if you want to fit in, choose a similar dress code.

When we meet someone, we have seven seconds to make a first impression. It's essential to be positive about yourself and not overly modest or self-deprecating. If you find it difficult to talk about yourself in a constructive manner, prepare a few paragraphs about yourself and list all of the things that you have done recently. If you do this after the passion and ambition exercises, you will find the right examples and be able to frame them in a positive light. The aim is not to lie or pretend to be something we are not. We are merely revealing with confidence who we are to other people.

Social Media

Like it or not, social media is where people are, and it is here to stay for the foreseeable future. We need to understand that social media is not a replacement for social interaction. While social media undeniably provides entertainment and an element of connection, it will eventually lead to dissatisfaction and unhappiness if you don't get out there and meet people physically. A study of Facebook users found that the amount of time they spent on the social network was inversely related to how happy they felt throughout the day.

Equally important to realise is that almost everything that people share on social media is edited. People will typically present the best possible perspective of their lives that they want others to see, and for good reason. Social media is where people turn to for entertainment, so many people feel the need to embellish their social pages accordingly.

As in real life, keep negativity on social networks to a minimum. We all feel annoyed and frustrated from time to time, but don't use social media to share these sentiments. In five years, whatever bothered you will be long forgotten; however, if you post about it on social media, there is a chance that it will still be visible years later. A good test is to ask yourself if you would be comfortable with your children or your mother seeing your post.

In the early days of separation, use social media to see what people are doing, to get in touch and to arrange physical meetups. Facebook, from my point of view, has less to do with your friends and more to do with groups. Groups of close friends usually chat on messenger services such as WhatsApp rather than on Facebook.

Facebook groups are typically a loose association of people who share common interests. So, for example, if you enjoy running, you can find a multitude of groups based on geographical area, distance or ambition. Facebook monitors your activity and then cleverly uses algorithms to recommend other groups and events.

As a tool, social media can be beneficial, if only to fill in your Tinder profile. When you are ready to start dating, you will need to understand the rules, including how to use social media.

Summary

Being separated provides many opportunities to be more social. It's absolutely imperative that you reach out to friends and extend your social network. Discover your passions to identify ways to spend your time doing something that you love with like-minded people.

Having a positive outlook and surrounding yourself with positive individuals is essential for your health and success. Positive people will help and encourage you to achieve your goals. But be aware that not all of your family and friends will share your enthusiasm.

Some people don't want you to change. Sometimes, it's because they are trying to protect you. Other times, it's because your initiative reflects on their lack of ambition. Don't try to justify yourself if you are faced with opposition or disapproval. Just know why it happens and focus on your goals.

Being more social and staying positive require mastery of your inner game. By adopting the right mindset, you will gain the confidence to be open, the willingness to engage with people in a social setting and the courage to dream big and follow your ambitions.

CHAPTER 9:
NAVIGATING THE WORLD OF DATING

In the not-so-distant future, a day will come when you suddenly realise that you have made it through to the other side. Life might still have its challenges, and your situation might not be perfect, but you will know that you are over the worst, and you will feel that you can handle anything that's thrown your way.

You will feel optimistic about the future, and you'll begin to have thoughts about the type of person you might like to share this future with. Welcome back to the world of dating.

Right at the start of this book, I encouraged you to work on yourself before the commencement of any new relationship. You must have the right mindset in order to avoid pursuing women simply to make yourself feel good. Otherwise, you will come across as needy and insecure.

Instead of looking for someone to make you feel good, focus on making other people feel good. By doing so, you will attract people to you.

So, what are women looking for in a man? Movie-star good looks? A chiselled body? A big, fat bank account? For some, yes, but fortunately for the rest of us, research repeatedly shows that these qualities are not women's top priorities.

Women are attracted to strength. They want someone who can care for and protect them, someone who can handle any given situation. Women are also drawn to drive and passion. They want to be with a man who is going places and who demonstrates potential. They want a man who plays full out, who is decisive and committed and who doesn't sit on the fence.

Women want a man who is passionate about life, who is a joy to be around, who is inspiring. They want a man who is compassionate, honest and caring. A man who has a good sense of humour and who is spontaneous. In short, women are looking for a real man who displays all of the characteristics that you have hopefully been developing throughout this book.

Improving How You Look

While model looks aren't critical, most women are not attracted to poorly presented men. Any man can improve his looks with better grooming. The image that you project should demonstrate that you belong to the same segment of society as the women that you are interested in or are interested in visiting. Men wearing humorous "I'm with stupid" t-shirts are a group that few women would aspire to. However, most women would like to at least visit a tattooed rock star.

Many of us have been brought up with the belief that focusing on the clothes we wear is superficial or narcissistic. This is simply not true. Caring about what we wear and how we present ourselves communicates that we have standards.

Maintaining our physical appearance signals that we have control over our lives. How we do anything is how we do everything. Neglecting to take care of the way we look indicates that other parts of our life might need work too.

That said, fashion can be a minefield. Do some market research, read magazines and search online for some ideas based on the market segment that you want to belong to. Fashionbeans.com is entertaining and comprehensive and Thread.com is especially useful because it gives you recommendations based on previous images that you liked.

Observe people in the street. Notice who looks good and who doesn't, and, more importantly, figure out why. Do their clothes match and complement each other? Are their clothes worn in the right way?

Go through your wardrobe and try everything on. If any item doesn't fit or if you haven't worn it in six months, sell it or donate it to a charity store. Be disciplined with yourself.

If your clothes are worn, give them away. If they are good quality, fit well and can be repaired, get them repaired. Your goal is to have a wardrobe that you can go to for any event, a wardrobe that you know has items that fit well and will help you look the part.

If you need new clothes, aim to buy wardrobe staples in the best quality you can afford. Good quality clothes can last for years if they are well looked after. Buying cheap, disposable fashion can seem like a better option, but those clothes tend not to last.

If you haven't already, join a gym. Most will provide a free consultation to measure your current level of fitness and develop a programme for you to follow. Combined with a healthy diet, this new fitness regimen will help you lose excess fat and build muscle mass. If you get in shape, virtually all clothes will look great on you.

Now that you've got the clothes ironed out, it's time to evaluate the rest of your body. Take a look at the list below for ideas to improve your image:

- Change your hairstyle
  Study the haircuts of actors, musicians and models in fashion magazines. Find a hairstyle that you like, and bring a photo of it to a quality hair salon. Ask the hairdresser to tell you how to style it at home, and buy the necessary styling products.

- Look after your teeth
  Brush your teeth at least twice a day, and make sure to floss. Go to the dentist for a regular check-up, and visit the hygienist at least twice a year. If your teeth are stained, consider whitening. Forget whitening toothpastes available in supermarkets; they don't work. Your dentist can make a mould of your teeth and provide you with a whitening solution. However, this is expensive and not the most effective option. Whitening strips made for the American domestic market are much more effective and are available online at a fraction of the cost of bespoke moulds.

- Look after your skin
  Wash your face with soap specially formulated for your face. Tone and moisturise as well. If you visit the larger chemists or department stores, they will give you free consultations and free samples of different products. Try a few until you find one

that you like. If you want to really spoil yourself, book yourself a facial. Did you think that only women get facials? Think again. A facial is the ultimate in relaxation, and I've never met a man who regretted having one.

- Get a tan
  Get outdoors as much as possible and get some colour in your skin. Not only will being outdoors give you a healthy glow, but it will also give you a much-needed boost of vitamin D, an essential micronutrient for healthy bones. Just make sure to protect your skin with sunscreen. Lobster red is not a look to aim for.

  In the winter, visit the tanning salon for a sunbed. I hear from some men that a spray tan works well. I've not tried it myself, but if it works, why not? I won't tell anyone.

- Lose the glasses
  Unless you rock eyewear like Jeff Goldblum, it might be time to upgrade your glasses or consider getting contacts or having laser eye surgery. I only need glasses for reading, so I was amazed that I could wear contacts for this. You can purchase varifocal contacts or wear a single lens for reading.

- Remove excess hair
  Ubiquitous on most high streets are salons and pop-up kiosks that perform threading. Threading is a quick and effective method of tidying eyebrows. At the very least, get some tweezers and remove the stray hairs yourself from between your eyebrows and down the outside of your eyes.

  Use the thin nozzle on a hair trimmer to remove the hair from your nostrils and in your ears. You can also buy wax kits from the chemist that remove the hair from your nostrils. This procedure is not as painful as it sounds. Also, make sure that you keep the hair on the back of your neck neat.

  Buy a hair trimmer with different blades so that you can trim the hair on different parts of your body. We don't live outdoors in caves anymore, so we can lose some of the hair.

- Get a manicure and pedicure
  You can't walk down a high street these days without falling over a nail salon. Enter any of these salons; they all welcome men too. Don't worry, they won't force you to choose a nail colour. You can have a clear top coat instead. Once inside, don't be surprised to find yourself chatting with all of the women in there. Visiting a nail salon will open up a new world for you. If you prefer to maintain your nails yourself, make sure that you keep them short, neat and clean.

Social Media and Dating Apps

Almost 40% of relationships in the UK and the US begin online. First impressions count online as they do in real life, so you must have suitable pictures. If you don't post a picture of yourself on your profile, potential dates will just scroll past.

Depending on the site, aim for a minimum of three pictures. One picture should be a relatively close up shot of your face. The second should be a full-length picture of your entire body. Women want to know what they are getting.

Don't be tempted to hide anything. If you do and you later meet someone on a date, the situation will likely be pretty uncomfortable for both of you. I remember meeting a date who had been creative with her profile pictures and had lied about her age. Looks aren't everything, of course, but I still felt duped, which tarnished my opinion of her.

Your pictures need to demonstrate that you are a great guy with an active social life. You must have at least one image of you alone. And no, an old picture with your wife cropped out will not do. You also want to have at least one picture of you in a group having a great time.

This concept is called social proof. If women can see that you are having fun with other people, they will conclude that you have high value and are worth being around. Even better, post a picture of you in an aspirational location, such as a foreign city, or a picture of you taking part in a sporting event.

Even if you are not using a dating app, you still need a social media presence where all of the above applies. If you meet a woman who is interested in you, the first thing she will do is search for your name online to see what she can discover about you.

If you don't have a social media presence, now is the time to create one. If you do have one, now is the time to review it. Evaluate the content and make sure that you are still happy to be associated with it. How you are now might be entirely different from how you were 10 years ago.

Once you start conversing with an interested woman, your objective is to move from the dating app to another messaging app as quickly as possible. Doing so will allow you to communicate better and showcase your personality.

Apps such as Tinder restrict communication, so by using messaging services such as WhatsApp, you can send images, videos, and sound as well as voice and text messages to give her a broader sensory experience.

Start slowly and don't be too quick to respond. A point of reference is to match her response time or respond slightly slower. As the frequency and response speed increases, match it.

An essential requirement for getting someone to like us is to establish frequent contact. But be careful not to cross the fine line into stalkerville. No matter what, never chase a response. If you have messaged her, she has received it, so there is no point in following up with a "just checking that you got my message." If she likes what she sees, she will respond. If she doesn't, move on. A low attachment is the name of the game in these early stages.

That said, if you are not receiving any interest or if your conversations keep fizzling out, you might need to review your approach. If you are not getting any attention, then your pictures and accompanying bio might need some work as well.

Make sure the pictures follow the guidelines above. Keep your bio brief, humorous and classy. Avoid anything too weird or cheesy. Just write something about you, your abilities and your interests. Here are some examples:

"Architect, HiiT junkie, loves sushi."

"Running and travelling addict."

"London based, former pro athlete."

"6' 6" in heels with a 5-star Uber rating."

"Frequent traveller, wanna join me?"

Once you have a match, initiate the conversation, but avoid opening with a simple "Hi" or "Hello." These openers won't get you noticed amongst all of the other men your match is chatting with.

Study her pictures and try to find something unique that you can open with. If she has a picture in Italy, for example, you could start with, "I see you've been to Rome. I loved it there. What's your favourite, pizza or pasta?"

If you are getting interest but can't keep the conversation going, you need to review your chat. Make sure it's casual and light. Ask questions and show interest in her. Tease her a little and keep her wanting more.

Don't let a conversation dry up. Instead, end it at its peak, giving a reason why you have to go that demonstrates your value. Be vague and say that you will message her later. The trick is to motivate her to want to come into your life, rather than inserting yourself into hers.

Once you feel that you've made a connection, ask if you can call her to arrange a date. If she doesn't show any signs of being interested, don't ask her. If the conversation isn't increasing in intensity, step back and let it go. She might not be that interested in you and might only see you as a form of amusement. By pushing away, her fear of missing out may crystallise a favourable opinion about you, and she may begin to pursue you.

Offline Dating

As useful as online dating apps are, there is a big, wide world out there full of women. Many people hide behind social media and dating apps. Some men feel fearful about approaching women directly. They worry that if they start talking to a woman, she will be dismissive and they will feel rejected. But what is the reality here? What is likely to happen in such a situation? The majority of us are social creatures. We like to feel good, so most people welcome meeting someone genuine, fun and interesting.

The worst-case scenario is that you will be politely declined. Sure, there are some people out there who might look down their nose at you, but their problem isn't you; it's them. Whenever someone reacts in this way, they always carry personal issues, so just be thankful that you've spotted a bad one and walk away.

I meet numerous people who are terrified of selling to other people. They have all sorts of strange beliefs, such as that selling is intrusive and somehow vulgar and unpleasant. I look at it differently: if you have a great product that will genuinely make someone's life better, you are doing them a disservice if you don't sell it to them.

Relationships are the same. When you have a great product like you, you are doing the women out there a disservice by not engaging them. Remember, women have the same fears: they want to talk to you, but the fear of rejection is holding them back. Why not help them out?

Building Confidence to Talk to Anyone without Fear

I know that it sounds like I'm stating the obvious, but the best way to overcome any fear is to face it. When we come face to face with our fears, we tend to find that our worries about what will happen are much worse than the reality.

What follows are three safe and straightforward exercises to help you become comfortable initiating conversations with other people. Start with someone you feel relaxed with, but continue challenging yourself until you can eventually speak with the type of woman you might want a relationship with.

1. Make small talk with 10 strangers. The goal is simply to start a conversation. If small talk doesn't come naturally to you, choose a topic such as the weather or news.

2. To challenge yourself further, make small talk with 10 strangers, but this time, make a note of their eye colour. There is no need to write it down; just make a mental note. Making eye contact is essential to connecting deeply with someone.

3. Give 10 people you meet a compliment. The compliment should be sincere and specific. A "you look nice" won't do. You might comment on an item of clothing they are wearing, their positivity or their sense of humour. The purpose of this exercise is to increase your interest and awareness of the people around you and to practice showing honest appreciation.

Preparing Your Approach

You must prepare yourself before making your approach. In any social encounter, highest energy wins. Your energy level should be equal to or slightly higher than that of the woman you're approaching. Most people want to have fun, so if you can bring a pleasant attitude, you will be welcomed. On the other hand, if you are a mood hoover, people will walk away irrespective of how good-looking you are.

Smile with your full face, talk more loudly than usual and project energy and enthusiasm through your voice and body. Remember the Bragging Exercise from Chapter 3? That activity works well to prepare you for this challenge.

Don't initiate the conversation with an apology such as, "Excuse me." This makes you sound insecure and unsure of yourself. A man of high status never apologises for his presence. Similarly, make sure your physical appearance doesn't betray insecurity.

Commit to the interaction and position yourself at a close, comfortable distance to her. Do not hover on the periphery. If she backs away, you know you've come too close, so maintain the new distance unless she starts to move in.

You can be direct and show a romantic interest straight away, but your chances of success will be lower. Think of it as a game.

When it's easy, there is less satisfaction compared to when you really had to earn a win. Your approach should be the same, so don't lower your value and make it too easy.

A better approach is to start the conversation based on an observation about the situation you both find yourself in. For example, if you are both waiting to enter a circuits class at the gym, you could ask what exercises they do in the class.

A solid approach will naturally lead to other topics of conversation, allowing you to get a feel for each other. Demonstrate your personality and self-worth, but don't try too hard. If she senses that you are looking to impress her or that you are seeking validation, she will perceive you as needy and find it to be a turnoff.

If she likes you, she will display some of the following signals:

- She approaches you
- She asks for your name
- She keeps touching you accidentally or meaningfully
- She asks a lot of questions about you
- She laughs at all of your jokes
- She teases and makes fun of you
- She moves into your personal space
- She draws attention to her neck and shoulders by playing with her hair or touching her skin

These signs are subtle, so don't immediately dive in just because you've spotted one. Instead, increase your awareness and look for others. You can also test her to see if she reacts positively. For instance, if she is asking you a lot of questions and has moved into your personal space, move away slightly while still engaging her to see if she follows you.

Once you feel that you've made a connection, ask for her phone number to arrange a date. If she isn't showing any signs of interest, don't ask her.

Don't end the conversation as soon as you have exchanged phone numbers, because it will make the interaction feel transactional. You don't want her walking away feeling that your sole objective was to get her number because she may feel used. Continue the conversation for another minute or so and then say goodbye. Take the lead and demonstrate that you have places you need to be.

Phone Calls

There are no rules on when you should call. You have to strike a balance between too soon and coming across as desperate and so long that she's forgotten who you are.

If you call and she doesn't answer, show confidence and leave a message. Tell her that you will try her again later. If she doesn't answer the second time, leave a message, but this time tell her to call you back.

Don't leave a message or start a phone call with a submissive introduction. Saying it's "just me" or something similar reduces your status.

If this is your first phone call with her, you need to break the ice. As soon as you've said hello, lead with a short story. It can be anything: something that happened to you today, where you currently are – it doesn't really matter. The objective is to try to make her laugh and feel relaxed.

Smile when you are talking to her, as it will come through in your voice. It might help to ready yourself ahead of the call by putting yourself into a positive, energetic state. Talk clearly and calmly but convey an upbeat tone. You want her to feel excited when she talks to you.

Ask her what she has been doing today and then make plans for your date. Don't be too available and do not drop another commitment for her. Remember, you are bringing her into your life, not dropping your life for her.

Before you ask her on a date, make sure you have a plan. There is nothing worse than securing a date and then asking the woman what she wants to do. She is looking for you to take the lead and demonstrate your value. This doesn't mean dining at an expensive restaurant. In fact, I would advise against flashing money around, because it sends the wrong impression and attracts the wrong type of woman.

Take her to a fresh, new bar or a pop-up restaurant. Aim for something that she hasn't done or experienced before. You want to make her life more exciting by being with you.

If she can't make a date for this week, tell her that you might be free on a particular day the week after. If she isn't sure that she is available, say that you will call her again next week. Be vague about when you will call to create anticipation.

Whether you have arranged a date or not, do not end the call straight away. As you did when you were talking face to face, continue chatting for a minute before finishing the call. Otherwise, she may feel some buyer's remorse.

If you are still not able to secure a date the following week, reconsider your approach. It doesn't matter how busy someone is, if they really wanted to meet you, they would make time for it. Did you portray a high enough status and social value? Did you look the part? What is your social media feed saying about you? Identify any areas of weakness and improve on them.

Going on a Date

Once you are on a date, it's your personality more than anything else that will motivate her to see you again. To be successful, you must be comfortable in your own skin, which is why we focused on these areas at the beginning of the book.

Confidence and happiness shine through in our words, tone of voice and body language. A positive frame of mind will influence your brain to automatically search for more positivity to support your feelings.

When you talk with someone, your mind will look to assign positive thoughts that will come through in your dialogue. Being a bit negative and cheeky about something can be fun, but people ultimately want to be around people who make them feel good.

You also need to build rapport. There are many techniques to do this, but we will focus on a simple one. Adopt the mindset that you have known the other person for years and that you really like each other. When you think like this, you will naturally be more relaxed and less uptight.

Rapport is a two-way process. If you want her to open up, you need to open up too. You cannot pretend to create rapport and keep yourself closed off; it just won't work.

To create genuine rapport, you must be fearless enough to let your guard down and talk openly. Revealing your own vulnerabilities is often the key to unlocking someone else's heart. Listen to what she is saying and try to understand how she really feels.

Be strong and demonstrate your strength, and I don't mean by flexing your muscles. Women want to be with a man who can protect them and look after them – it's basic human nature. She needs to see that you can look after yourself and others, that you are honourable and trustworthy and that you are decisive and self-assured.

If you usually struggle to decide what to eat on a menu, go online and read the menu beforehand. Decide on what you will eat rather than dither on the date. Ask what she would like and order for both of you. This act demonstrates strength and status.

Your relationship history will invariably come up in conversation. Your date is trying to decide if she can see a future with you, so be prepared for questions such as:

- Why are you single?
- What was your ex-partner like?
- What was your relationship like?
- What went wrong?
- Do you have children?
- How often do you see your children?
- Are you divorced?

Prepare an account that presents you in a positive light while not being overtly negative about your ex-partner. Also, be aware of what you don't say. Lying by omission is when a person leaves out important information or fails to correct a pre-existing misconception in order to hide the truth. Quite often, we can dress this up as a white lie to justify our actions, but the fact remains that it is still a lie.

I fell foul of this myself. When I started dating, I was worried that any sensible woman would run for the hills if she knew I was still married, even though my divorce was being processed.

I met someone, and early on, I became aware that she understood me to be divorced, but I didn't correct her. As the relationship developed, it played on my mind, and I had to confess. Although she was understanding about it, her trust in me was clearly affected.

After that, I made a point of explaining my status at the appropriate moment. I felt it was better to be upfront and allow the other person to make an informed decision rather than mislead them. In any case, my concerns were totally unfounded. If you communicate well and are honest, you have nothing to worry about.

Summary

The secret to dating success starts before you even meet a woman. It starts from within. Knowing what you want and living your passions gives you a positive outlook on life. Focus on creating the best life for yourself rather than rushing into a new relationship. A relationship should be an addition to your amazing life, not your whole life.

When you are ready, meet lots of people and go on many dates. Be courteous: hold doors open, sit down last, walk on the outside of the pavement. Some people may think that these are outdated practices, but they are just good manners. You have nothing to fear if you are thoughtful and respectful. Be chivalrous, be authentic and, above all, have fun!

CHAPTER 10:
WHAT'S NEXT FOR YOU?

We have been on quite the journey together, in what is a difficult time for any man. I thank you for taking the time to read this book, and I hope that the stories and experiences I've shared have shown you that regardless of your current situation, life will get better and be better.

As more people became aware that I was writing this book, men began reaching out to me for advice. The question they all asked me was whether the stress and aggravation that they were experiencing would ever end. Some men are so worn down by their circumstances that they can't see a way out. Others try to ignore the situation until they are forced to take action, before putting their heads in the sand once again.

When life is beating us like this, we find it difficult to look to the future. But we must. Life ebbs and flows; it has ups and downs. We can't control what life throws at us, but we can control how we deal with our circumstances. This mindset is a central theme throughout the book, which I hope you will use to your advantage. Doing so will have a profound effect on your life, both now during this challenging period and throughout the rest of your life.

It is no coincidence that we began the book by focusing on the inner game and that we revisited this approach throughout. Your inner game is the most critical factor to help you successfully negotiate the challenges of divorce and separation. From letting go and creating a new type of relationship with your ex-partner to finding and dating a new woman, having the right mindset is essential for success.

If you follow the advice in this book and implement the processes, you will not only start to feel better, but you will also come through the ordeal happier, stronger and healthier. Implementation, actually taking action, is the key, so to facilitate this, I have created a checklist below to keep you on track.

I sincerely wish you all the best, and I look forward to hearing your success stories. You can reach me at james@ realmansdivorce.com.

#1 Begin with the end in mind.

- Decide what your objectives are. Your objectives should influence every decision you make, helping you make the right decisions for the long term and, more importantly, helping you avoid making mistakes.
- Put temporary arrangements in place until you finalise the details of the separation; for example, living arrangements, division of assets and liabilities, child maintenance and access to bank accounts.

#2 Everything starts from within.

- List everything that you must do and prioritise. You will have a host of things to deal with. Creating the list will not only increase your productivity so that you can get through the tasks but also reduce the chances of you becoming overwhelmed.
- Work out what went wrong, and think about how you contributed to the breakup. Apologise if you need to and then let go. The process allows you to close the door on the past, knowing that you will avoid the same mistakes in future relationships.
- Complete the values exercise to understand your motivations and what is important to you. Live your life congruent with your values.
- Practice the gratitude exercise daily to boost your mood and put you in a positive frame of mind. This will enable you to tackle the challenges ahead and be receptive to opportunities.
- Wake up each morning and choose to enjoy and make the most out of the next 1440 minutes.

#3 When emotions are high, intelligence is low.

- Overhaul how you manage communications. Take control over your phone; don't let your phone control you.
- Review how you communicate with your ex-partner. Make sure that your words and body language support each other. Practice active listening and be assertive. Be mindful of the power of your words.
- Rehearse difficult conversations and identify and find solutions for any objections you may face.
- Be clear on what you want and what is unacceptable to define your negotiation range. Actively listen to understand your ex-partner's needs and motivations. Seek to find solutions and aim for win-win.
- Recognise the physical feelings of anger. If you are prone to anger, come up with a strategy to silence it.
- If you find yourself in or entering into an argument, ask yourself the following questions:
  - Why am I engaging in this argument?
  - What do I want to achieve from it?
  - How am I going to do that?
  - How likely will I achieve my goal?
  - What are the risks?

#4 Put your children first.

- Establish regular contact with your children as soon as possible. Let them know when you will see them again and where you will live. If contact is restricted, keep calm, and play the long game. Do not do anything that could legally jeopardise access to your children.
- Focus on how you can be a positive influence in your children's lives rather than wasting your energy on negativity and what you cannot control.
- Complete the parenting plan to document how you and your children's mum will care for your children.

- Think quality, not quantity, and make the most of every minute with your children. Be fun, and provide guidance, encouragement and love.

#5 Conflict makes the cash register sing.

- Agree on the reasons for your divorce with your wife and process the divorce yourself.
- When using solicitors, make sure that they are aligned with your strategy and optimise your time with them by being prepared.
- Try to informally agree on the details of the financial settlement with your ex-partner. Take your time and don't give everything away. Put temporary arrangements in place where necessary. Make sure to use a solicitor to draft the financial consent with a clean break clause for court approval.
- Develop a working relationship with your ex-partner and informally agree on access to your children to avoid costly and ineffective legal proceedings.

#6 Take control of your finances and safeguard your future.

- Use the child maintenance service formula to calculate how much child maintenance you should pay. Ensure that you have a temporary agreement in place until you decide with your ex-partner the final method of calculation.
- Use your income and outgoings to create a budget. Aim for your necessities to be no more than 70% of your total income. Look for ways to reduce your expenses and debt.
- Use the money management strategy to plan for your future and sever your reliance on credit facilities.
- Calculate your net worth to help you with the financial settlement with your ex-partner and to help you make more strategic financial decisions.

#7 Raise your heart rate and smiles.

- Reduce your consumption of processed foods and red meat. Learn to cook, and eat more vegetables and fruit. Drink at least two litres of water each day.
- Aim for at least 150 minutes of exercise per week doing activities that you enjoy.
- Make sure that you are getting sufficient sleep to allow your body to repair itself and to boost testosterone production.

#8 Our potential is determined by our ambitions.

- Identify your passions and fill your time doing what you love.
- Get clarity on your ambitions and focus on achieving what you genuinely want from life.
- Be more social. Reach out to people, make new friends and use visualisation techniques to prepare for social events.

#9 Make other people feel good.

- Get your head right before entering another relationship. Create a life that women want to be part of rather than chasing to be part of a woman's life.
- Improve how you look. The more areas that you improve, the better you will feel.
- Use social media and dating apps to your advantage, but don't hide behind them.
- Practice the confidence exercises to learn to talk to anyone.
- Be authentic, honest and chivalrous.
- Above all, have fun.

APPENDIX

Parenting Plan

The parenting plan demonstrates both parents' commitment to putting the needs of their children first. It enables both parents to be fully involved in all critical aspects of decision-making and childcare.

The parenting plan is a framework. Not every consideration needs to be resolved before implementing the plan. Instead, the plan seeks to keep the focus firmly on the practical considerations of childcare by separating it from the conflicts that frequently accompany divorce or separation.

Parent A.

```

```

Parent B.

```

```

Children's Names

```

```

Section 1. Living Arrangements
Weekdays (Monday – Friday)

Which days and nights will the children stay with each parent?

```

```

What are the school-run arrangements? Drop off and collection times?

```
┌────────────────────────────────────────────────────┐
│                                                    │
│                                                    │
│                                                    │
└────────────────────────────────────────────────────┘
```

Do the children attend any after-school clubs? Who is responsible for drop off and collection?

```
┌────────────────────────────────────────────────────┐
│                                                    │
│                                                    │
│                                                    │
└────────────────────────────────────────────────────┘
```

Weekends

How will the weekends be shared between parents? Alternate weekends? Each weekend shared? How will bank holidays be divided?

```
┌────────────────────────────────────────────────────┐
│                                                    │
│                                                    │
│                                                    │
└────────────────────────────────────────────────────┘
```

What are the collection arrangements for the weekend? Collect from school on Friday? Collect from home on Saturday? What are the drop-off arrangements?

```
┌────────────────────────────────────────────────────┐
│                                                    │
│                                                    │
│                                                    │
└────────────────────────────────────────────────────┘
```

What are the arrangements for any scheduled weekend event? Clubs, activities, parties?

```
┌────────────────────────────────────────────────────┐
│                                                    │
│                                                    │
│                                                    │
└────────────────────────────────────────────────────┘
```

Section 2. Holidays and Special Days

School Holidays

What are the arrangements for the half-term holiday?

What are the arrangements for the Easter holiday?

What are the arrangements for the summer holiday?

What are the childcare arrangements for days when neither parent is available to look after the children? Who is responsible for organising?

What are the arrangements for each parent to take the children out of the country during the holidays?

Christmas

What are the arrangements for Christmas?

How will we accommodate family traditions into our arrangements? Christmas plays, carol service, family gatherings?

How will we communicate regarding gifts?

Children's Birthdays

What are the arrangements? Both organise and attend? Separate celebrations? How will the presents be arranged?

Mother's Day / Father's Day

What are the arrangements? Always schedule the weekend with the appropriate parent? Split the weekend? Will we each organise gifts with the children?

Other Special Days / Events

Are there any other days that we need to consider? What are the arrangements?

Section 3. Practical Considerations

Travel and Handover

How will the children travel from one parent to the other? Is this shared or predominately the responsibility of one parent? Do we need to agree in advance or can we be flexible?

What are the details of these arrangements? Location? Time? What clothes and other belongings will be taken and returned at handover?

Contact with the Non-Resident Parent

What are the arrangements for the children to contact the parent they are not with? Telephone or video calls? Do the calls need to be scheduled or can we be flexible? Are there times that are not convenient?

Contact with Other Family Members

When will the children see grandparents and other prominent family members?

Rules and Routines

What routines do we agree are essential to be maintained across both homes? Bedtime, mealtimes, homework, screen time?

What rules do we agree are essential to be maintained across both homes? Internet and social media access, staying out late, manners?

How do we discipline our children?

```



```

Section 4. Communication

How will we communicate with each other? Phone? Messenger? Email? Are there times that are not appropriate to call?

```



```

What parenting decisions do we need to consult with each other?

```



```

How will we share relevant information about the children with each other?

```



```

How will we behave in front of the children?

```



```

How will we settle disputes?

What do we do if one of us is unable to meet their obligations from the Parenting Plan?

How will we introduce new partners into our children's lives?

Section 5. Education

How will we get involved separately as parents at the school?

How will we work together to make decisions on school or course selections and further education?

Section 6. Health

Who organises routine health issues?

What do we do in case of emergencies?

How do we manage time off work due to child sickness?

What are the arrangements if one of us dies?

Section 7. Finances

How will we share day-to-day costs for clothes, school trips and larger items such as computers?

What are the arrangements for pocket money?

What provisions will we put in place to support our children as they grow up? For example, college and university, the first car?

Section 8. Additional Business

Is there anything else that we want to capture that hasn't been included in another part of the Parenting Plan?

ACKNOWLEDGEMENTS

I always knew I had a book in me, I just needed to find a strong enough motivation and the encouragement to make it happen. To Phoebe and Rafe, you inspire me to be a better man, the best dad and the biggest kid I can be.

Thanks to Myron Golden, whose advice to start with dictation helped me to overcome the fear of the enormity of writing a book. Sedonia Thomas, for transcribing the first chapters and for your encouragement, which spurred me to keep going. Richard McMunn, Jordan and Joshua at How 2 Become, for your support and advice throughout this process. My editor, Marilyn Lapu, for fixing my grammar, waffling and annoying habit of using two spaces after a full stop. And Natalie Rimmer, for her honesty and for creating my book cover design.

Finally, I want to give a big thanks to all of those people who have made my life so colourful – you know who you are. To my friends and family, who continue to support me on my various endeavours, and to those closest to me, who see me at my best and worst and still love me.